Writings on Wright

The MIT Press
Cambridge, Massachusetts
London, England

Writings on Wright

Selected Comment on Frank Lloyd Wright

Edited, with introduction and commentary,
by H. Allen Brooks

This book was set in VIP Univers by Graphic Composition, Inc. and printed and bound by Halliday Lithograph in the United States of America.

Library of Congress Cataloging in Publication Data
Main entry under title:

Writings on Wright.

Bibliography: p.
Includes index.
1. Wright, Frank Lloyd, 1867–1959—Addresses, essays, lectures. I. Brooks, H. Allen (Harold Allen), 1925–
NA737.W7W76   720'.92'4   81–8438
ISBN 0–262–02161–7   AACR2

His architecture is not in the current of the present regime any more than Walt Whitman's writings were in the current of the Gilded Age: hence his value is not that he has dominated the scene and made it over in his image, but that he has kept the way open for a type of architecture which can come into existence only in a much more humanized and socially adept generation than our own.

Lewis Mumford, 1929

Contents

Contents

Contents

Acknowledgments

Much of what usually appears in a preface will be found in the introduction—questions concerning my objectives, criterion, and editorial policy. That leaves only acknowledgments to be offered here. Yet when a book has seen some six summers of intermittent work, the number of people sharing time and talent, particularly in the decision-making process, is too large for inclusion on this page. These people are remembered, however, and to each I express my gratitude. A more specific list would comprise those authors whose writings appear here, for without them and their magnificent cooperation this book would not have been. Then, too, there are the photographs, not many but sought with special care. John Glover offered time and care in preparing prints, Henry-Russell Hitchcock and the Museum of Modern Art kindly put their resources at my service, and various individuals—as specifically noted—permitted reproduction of their work. Ben Raeburn furnished valued counsel on the texts.

Introduction

This is not a typical anthology. It is not meant to be. Rather it is a book deeply concerned with the reality and myth of Frank Lloyd Wright—about people's perceptions of Wright and his work. It is not a hefty compendium of historic documents, nor the usual architectural history, nor a recounting of the endless legends about him. The latter, in fact, is precisely what this book seeks to expose and correct; to dispel fable and attempt to reveal the truth, thereby gaining a greater understanding of Wright's architecture but also of the man himself as well as his place vis-à-vis the times in which he lived.

What, then, was my concept for this book, what principles guided my selection? Originally my aim was simply to assemble the most quoted, the most often footnoted, writings on Wright—but when I had done so I found that these once insightful texts (especially those that explored Wright's artistic sources) had lost pertinence with the passage of time, due to their themes becoming assimilated into our general knowledge. This is why few of these writings are included here, even though it regretfully means omitting the seminal research of some of our finest scholars.* Another reason for their absence is that these early studies of influences represent but a first, tentative step toward a deeper understanding. Wright is too elusive, too profound to be so easily explained.

---

* The most notable among these studies are (chronologically) Henry-Russell Hitchcock, "Frank Lloyd Wright and the 'Academic Tradition'" (1944); Dimitri Tselos, "Exotic Influences in the Architecture of Frank Lloyd Wright" (1953); Grant C. Manson, "Wright in the Nursery: The Influence of Froebel Education on the Work of Frank Lloyd Wright" (1953); Vincent Scully, *The Shingle Style; Architectural Theory and Design from Richardson to the Origins of Wright* (1955). For complete references see the bibliographic note.
The influence of Wright upon others was also a topic of investigation; see particularly Nikolaus Pevsner, "Frank Lloyd Wright's Peaceful Penetration of Europe" (1939); Henry-Russell Hitchcock, "Wright's Influence Abroad" (1940); Vincent Scully, "Wright vs. the International Style" (1954). These likewise are omitted from the present volume.

The ultimate question is not "from whom did he learn?" but "what did he achieve and [more significant] how did he achieve it?" And on these questions there is still a dearth of perceptive writing.

As finally conceived, therefore, my plan has been to omit much traditionally accepted writing in favor of documents that record people's actual relation to Wright—people with whom he actually lived, worked, and argued, not just the views of critics and historians whose existence he abided but the men and women who encountered Wright directly—who knew him in his own world and saw him in a way that the outside observer cannot. This, it is hoped, will bring a new dimension to Wright studies by avoiding a single point of view as well as a single type of writing. Friends, family, clients, co-workers, and homeowners present a vivid picture that no biographer, historian, journalist, or critic can hope to match. And, for the first time, this latter group is placed in a clear historical perspective, thereby revealing an ever evolving interpretation of Wright and his work—and, for that matter, of much architectural history and criticism during the first eighty years of this century. This legacy of critical comment has been culled not only from articles and books but from letters, diaries, newspapers, surveys, poems, and even broadcasts. When one realizes that the first English-language book on Wright did not appear until 1942, when Wright was already seventy-five, one appreciates the advantage of these comprehensive resources.

Though a collection of writings, this book is a very personal statement. The selections usually illustrate what I wished to say about Wright, that is why I chose them, but the words of others are often more authoritative than my own. Yet the picture presented, I believe, is not a distorted one except that it does not take into account the sometimes negative reactions to Wright that have, by and large, failed to find their way into print.

A word about the introductions preceding each of the individual texts. Their purpose is to provide biographical information, to give greater unity and direction to the whole, and to allow me to express my own comments and ideas. I have my own views on the significance of Frank Lloyd Wright, and you will find them here.

The organization of the book is thematic rather than chronological, although dates are often a governing factor. Part I
comments on Wright the man, as seen by his friends, family,
and contemporaries; it concerns his life-style and personality.

Part II introduces Wright's clients and co-workers, and also his
buildings, how they were designed, constructed, and (most
important) how they worked. The interaction between architect and client is discussed as is the owner's reaction to living
in a Wright-designed house. Myth has often shrouded these
matters, and any reader versed in these myths will find this
section a surprise, perhaps a revelation.

Parts III through V survey the broad spectrum of critical comment that accrued around Wright after 1900. These writings
fall naturally into three parts in a manner that is both unexpected and informative—and helps to explain why Wright was
so often antagonistic toward his critics. Part III spans the period from 1900 to 1912 when Wright's work was discovered,
discussed, and dismissed by his often unsympathetic country-
men. Except for friends and colleagues, there was scarcely a
writer in America who understood or praised his work. The
esteemed architectural critics of the day seemed at a loss for
what to say. And after 1912 they took the safest course, that of
saying nothing. A few East Coast architectural editors main-
tained an interest in Wright's career, but for nearly thirty years
they could hardly find a contributor on Wright for their columns—with the result that they were sometimes prompted to
ask Wright to write about himself.

By 1912, however, European architects had discovered Wright.
They learned of him through photographs in American magazines (especially Wright's own 1908 article in *Architectural
Record* entitled "In the Cause of Architecture") and through a
magnificent folio of 100 lithographs, drawn by Wright, that
was published in Berlin, Germany, by Ernst Wasmuth in 1910.
The following year Wasmuth published another, smaller volume containing photographs and plans. These events altered
the course of European architecture—and perhaps painting
and sculpture as well. Europe, not America, was ready for
Wright's ideas. Affected by Wright were such architects as
Gropius, Mies van der Rohe, Mendelsohn, Oud, Rietveld, Du-
dock, Wils, and many others from among the Expressionists

and International Style architects in Germany and the Amsterdam School and de Stijl groups in Holland. Most of these men grasped the significance of Wright's historic achievement—that of creating a radically new concept of interior space, a phrase that they introduced into the literature on Wright. From 1910 until World War II most of the perceptive comment on Wright originated among these Dutch, German, and, to a lesser extent, Swiss *architects* whose writings appear, often for the first time in English, in part IV.

Finally, as war approached, Wright was reclaimed by his fellow Americans. Slowly at first, but more rapidly after Wright's death in 1959 (at the age of 91), an ever broader range of American contributors entered the field (see particularly part II). Subsequent to the literature that analyzed Wright's artistic sources came full-length biographies, or occasionally an interpretive, analytical article such as appears in part V. Although Americans dominated the writing scene, English and Italian writers made important contributions too.

To conclude, a word about my editing of these texts. Many are greatly abridged. Originally I planned to insert ellipsis dots for each omission but their frequency was often disruptive; therefore they are not always used. Footnotes are deleted. Some titles are modified or changed in order to avoid the ubiquitous "Frank Lloyd Wright" but also to refocus the title after the abridgment of the text. Dates following the title refer to the year of publication; where two dates appear the first is the year being remembered and the second the year of publication. Full bibliographic references and copyright notices when applicable are at the bottom of each title page. Pagination for the articles lists pages in the unabridged version while that for books lists the location of the excerpts. A short bibliographic note appears at the back of the book. A chronological list showing the thirty-three items reprinted in this book follows this introduction. The distribution is fairly even over a period of eighty years.

Chronological List of Contents

Where two dates are separated by a virgule (/), the first is the date being recollected by the writer and the second the date of publication.

Writings on Wright

Part I

The Man: His Personality and Life-Style

Descriptions of Frank Lloyd Wright from his early years are short and very rare, and the few that exist come mostly from Europeans. At home there was less need to discuss the man, apart from his architecture, until late in life when he became a national celebrity and enjoyed widespread acclaim. His clients wrote of him (see part II), and their comments confirm what we observe from the following texts—that the private Wright was very different from the crusty, dominating, difficult to deal with personality that he often cultivated as his public image.

In 1887 Frank Lloyd Wright left Madison, Wisconsin, to seek his fortune as an architect in Chicago. He was nineteen—almost twenty. He already had a smattering of graphics and pre-engineering courses at the university as well as some practical experience behind him, but his real training took place in the Windy City, first with J. L. Silsbee, and then Adler & Sullivan with whom he stayed until 1893 when he entered private practice. In 1889 he married and built a home in suburban Oak Park where he lived, raising a family of six, until 1909. The house was constantly being expanded and redesigned with a studio

Writings on Wright

added in 1897. (This historic structure is now open to the public: The Frank Lloyd Wright Home & Studio Foundation, Forest Avenue, Oak Park, Illinois.)

Two Letters (1916)

C. R. Ashbee

The renowned arts and crafts designer, C. R. Ashbee, met Wright in 1900, and they became close friends. In 1909, Wright, beset with marital problems, left Oak Park and his family in order to sojourn in Europe, where he completed one hundred magnificent drawings that Ernst Wasmuth of Berlin published in 1910. He visited the Ashbees at Chipping Campden, England, en route home. While there he asked "C. R." to write the preface for a second book, consisting of photographs and plans, published by Wasmuth the following year.

Soon after returning to America, Wright settled near Spring Green, Wisconsin, where his forefathers had homesteaded and first cleared the land. He built for himself a new home, called Taliesin (Welsh for Shining Brow) and a new life. But tragedy soon struck (1914) when a deranged servant, axe in hand, set the house ablaze and murdered seven occupants as they fled the flames. Wright's life was spared (he was in Chicago supervising construction of Midway Gardens), but his domestic tranquillity was shattered for many years to come.

Previously unpublished letters printed with the kind permission of Felicity Ashbee.

Taliesin was rebuilt (as again after a fire in 1925), but the loss

of life was irreplaceable. The shock took its toll on Wright, and

this was evident to Ashbee when he visited in 1916, and wrote

these reflections to his wife.

February 25, 1916:

Frank himself has grown much older, his hair is quite grey and
though he is only forty-seven or there about one would take
him for fiftyish—even more. He came to meet me driving a
wild brown horse called 'Kaiser.' He was dressed in a sort of
buff leather suit—like the puritan fathers wore—with a long
black silk tie, and his long grey hair under a seal skin cap gave
him rather the look of a puritan, but of an earlier German generation such as Rembrandt might have drawn.

April 14, 1916:

[Taliesin, figures 13–15, has] a staff of thirty, men and women,
married and single, outdoor and indoor. They keep seven
horses, there's a farm and altogether a rather splendid establishment but quite unconventional, and very beautiful in its
bohemian and original way. They have planted vineyards to
make their own wine, and there are great orchards and gardens, a lake, a waterfall and generally what in England would
go to the Park of a Grand Seigneur. As for the House itself it
has many private rooms but two living rooms—one for music
and teaching, the other the print room where we look at Hiro-
shige and Utamaro—the choicest Yoshiwara drawings. From
all the windows there are superb views over the Wisconsin
river, and the landscape this week has been tender with silver
birch against the russet oak, the earthy pink flush of sumac,
dark green cedar and flashes of pale blue sky and river
through it all.

A Visit with Wright (1924)

Eric Mendelsohn

The era of the prairie house, brilliantly captured in Wasmuth's publications, was at an end when the German architect Eric Mendelsohn visited Wright at Taliesin in 1924. The previous decade had seen Wright build Midway Gardens in Chicago, the Imperial Hotel in Tokyo, and complete several concrete block houses in southern California, of which Mrs. Millard's house, La Miniatura, was his favorite. Yet by the mid-twenties he had few commissions. His creative development, however, was far from stagnant; he was, in fact, experiencing a regenerative phase of immense importance for the future.

Taliesin, like the Oak Park house before it, continued to grow and change, as did the numerous outbuildings that eventually included a farm, school, theater, and thousands of acres of land along the Wisconsin River. It remained Wright's principal home for nearly half a century and became a mecca for visitors from around the world. Yet its future remains uncertain; one hopes some way to save it for posterity will be found.

Beyer, Oskar, ed. *Eric Mendelsohn: Letters of an Architect*, London, New York, Toronto: Abelard-Schuman, 1967, pp. 71–75

Chicago, November 5, 1924

Taliesin is his farm. Two hours from Milwaukee in the state of Wisconsin [figures 13–16].

Wright picked me up in Madison, Wisconsin's university town. One and a half hours by car on a warm, stormy evening. He is sixty-five [*sic*, 57]; so I am twenty years younger. But we were friends at once, bewitched by space, holding out our hands to one another in space; the same road, the same goal, the same life, I believe.

I brought him the greetings of the whole of the young movement in Europe—to him, the father, the champion.

We are at Taliesin, high up on the hill. It was a fantastic entry—into his house, to be his guest, the friend of this unbelievably rich imagination.

I was very much moved by these surroundings. A wonderful room—windows all around—in yellow, brown and gold with Japanese ornaments; and a view over farm, high ground, valley and river.

He showed me his house with subdued lighting, in its architectonic spaciousness, its gold colors and its Asiatic ornaments.

We ate a farm supper, a simple, patriarchal, country meal.

In the late evening we received the architects: Neutra, Moser, Canada, Japan, Armenia.

The two of us talked together, for ourselves in some measure. About the world of the future, architecture and religion.

Wright says that the architecture of the future—he sees it naturally from the viewpoint of his own work—is for the first time in history wholly architecture, space in itself, without any prescribed model, without embellishments—movement, in three and four dimensions.

He says that yellow is the color of creation, of the earth, of life, of death; gold is the highest life and blessedness after it.

A look at the morning, windy fresh, with autumn sharpness. A dream house, a spatial dream, a visionary master, a master.

Communal Sunday breakfast for the whole farm: father; guest; architects with their wives, mothers-in-law and babies; chauffeur and farm hands.

Bacon, cream and all the juiciness of this powerful vitality.

We let the exceptionally sunny day make up our minds for us: we took photographs and were carried swiftly along until midday.

Then I had to change into clothes like his: a fantastic garment with something Indian about it—more or less without buttons (which he detests). Bark shoes, a long staff, gloves and a tomahawk; and so we went up a marvelous road, to the surrounding hills, land that a hundred years ago was still no-man's-land. Now it is abandoned by the redskins and growing wild where it is not taken over by falling trees and landslides.

In a curve about us was the Wisconsin River; the two of us were ahead.

We climbed down to the beach, a broad expanse of sand, like dunes; for the water has receded considerably. We had a competition in the sand. Wright drew with angular lines a massive garage which he is working on at the moment, with a fantastic superstructure. I did a sketch with a rounded contour.

He drew ornaments spontaneously, circular and angular in contrast; interpreted them like a sage, like an actor! Poor constructivists!

An actor, that is one part of him. I said to Byrne, "Wright is seldom simple, without gestures. But he can be simple, quite simple. I have watched him, I have felt him, I know him."

Back up the hill again through the last, the very last glory of autumn. A moment of peace; a distant view of Taliesin, his home of old, his house.

In the evening: music, Victrola records, one after another. I went to the record cupboard and arranged the program. Whitman [sic, Whiteman?]—that is super-jazz—Bach—Whitman—Bach.

He was pleased. I had to draw. He wanted a "Bach vision."

I drew through the evening and next morning. He picked out the best sketches and the most finished. I had to sign it and write: "To the Master."

He radiated, radiantly filled with life and with the will for more open, hopeful years: the radiance of eternal life, of the generation to come, of his immortality.

This morning was a single song, a single Bach concert. I spent it at his desk with all the disorder of his orderly being.

We drove together to Madison along a yellow road through the fields. We enjoyed the sun and spoke little. He said I was the first European to come and seek him out and truly to find him. I said that people will ask, everyone will—and I shall say, "I have seen him, I was with him."

He said the same thing to me, out of courtesy and the wisdom of age—but I felt more; dream and purpose, happiness and hope. . . .

Where does he stand?

His origin is apparent, his genius beyond doubt, his road has only just begun. It is the road which youth must take, traveling with him and beyond him.

Profiles: The Prodigal Father (1930)

Alexander Woollcott

Alexander Woollcott visited Wright at Taliesin in 1925. This

was the year of the second Taliesin fire and the year when the

Dutch periodical Wendingen *devoted seven special issues to*

his work with contributions by many of the most distinguished

European architects of the day. These issues were then pub-

lished as a book: The Life-Work of the American Architect

Frank Lloyd Wright. *It was at this time that Richard Neutra and*

Werner Moser worked briefly with Wright at Taliesin, and

when Wright himself was much involved with experiments in

the use of circular and triangular forms (as opposed to the tra-

ditional right angular ones) as a basis for architectural design.

Today there is less, it seems to me, of the old disparity between the high honor in which Wright has long been held
abroad and the position which he was permitted—or let us say
encouraged—to occupy here at home. But consider, please,
the irony of that disparity in its heyday a few years ago. Here
was a native American being hailed overseas as the outstanding creative genius of our time in architecture—an artist
whose drawings were pored over and studied by every student in Europe, a pioneer who had profoundly influenced all
recent building in Germany and about whom the French and
the Dutch were publishing reverent volumes, a man of
achievement who had been all but canonized in Japan,

The New Yorker 6, July 19, 1930, pp. 22–25.

whence every year the Mikado still sends several small, dusky disciples to sit at the feet of this Wisconsin Gamaliel. The travel bureaus that guide European sightseers from Niagara Falls to the Mammoth Cave (just as they push Americans around Europe from Salisbury Cathedral to the Grand Canal) learned before long that they could satisfy some of their clients here only by organizing tours to the home and works of Frank Lloyd Wright. . . .

As I have said, there have been recent signs of America catching up with Wright. Princeton and Cornell have been summoning the alarming creature from Wisconsin to lecture to their young, and in May the Architectural League here in New York not only gave a breath-taking exhibition of his work, but followed it with an exuberant dinner in his honor. As he listened to the speeches, Wright, who has always rather enjoyed regarding himself as a bit of an Ishmaelite, must have experienced some of the disquieting emotions which recently perturbed the bosom of another stormy petrel of our time. I refer to one Bernard Shaw, to whom the British government, which he had so often rendered uneasy, proffered humbly and vainly not long ago a seat in the House of Lords. I am sure that both Shaw and Wright had an uncomfortable feeling that they were being honored as if they were already dead. . . .

I first saw Wright himself on an afternoon in 1925 when, on a lecture tour in the Middle West, I found myself in Madison and learned that Wright's own house at Spring Green was only fifty miles away. I wanted to see with my own eyes the home that such a man would build for himself. Taliesin—that means "Radiant Brow" in Welsh—was already famous. Wright had fashioned it out of the wood and stone he found in this valley where, for three generations, his people had lived, and where his toes remembered the very feel of the soil from the barefoot days of his boyhood . . . .

I had read enough of Wright's dicta on architecture—maxims, you might call them, and certainly some of them are silencers—and seen enough of his work to forecast the quality of Taliesin. I knew that it would pick up its colors from the red cedars, white birches, and yellow-sand limestone round about, that it would gratefully take its lines from the crest of the hill it was to crown, that indeed it would not be so much *on* the hill as *of* it. I knew that it would be peculiarly suitable to the landscape whence it sprang, and to the needs and habits of the man occupying it. I would not be equipped to discuss it in the technical terms of organic architecture, but I knew it would be different from all other houses in the world, without any of the visible and aching strain of a conscious effort to be different. Of course that is the peculiar gift of Wright and his like in this world—to build freshly as though we had all just come out of Eden with no precedents to tyrannize over us. I knew therefore that in Taliesin I would find nothing alien, nothing automatic, nothing unreasonable. . . .

All this I expected, but I had not enough gift of divination to realize in advance how inexpressibly consoling would be its every aspect, how happily would the house grow like a vine on that hill-crest, how unerringly would every window foresee and frame the landscape that was to croon to the man within, above all how pliantly the unpretentious home would meet halfway the participation of the countryside. Why, if a lovely tree was in the way of that house, the house just doffed its cap respectfully and went around it.

I spent two wondering hours at Taliesin. A sunset storm was gathering in the west as I drove away. Next morning in Minneapolis I read that, within an hour after I had left, lightning had struck the house and burned it to the ground. . . .

I know how flagrantly he himself had invited some of the thunderbolts that have struck him. I know what perverse and tactless mockery of all who would serve him dances ever in his eyes. I know how near the surface, always, is the untamed imp in him that bids him upset the very apple cart he is hungrily approaching. But I think, too, that no one in the modern world has brought to architecture so good a mind, so leaping an imagination, or so fresh a sense of beauty. Indeed, if the editor of this journal were so to ration me that I were suffered to apply the word "genius" to only one living American, I would have to save it up for Frank Lloyd Wright.

Frank Lloyd Wright (1939)

Anonymous

*During the 1930s Wright turned increasingly to the spoken and
written word. His lectures at Princeton University in 1930 soon
appeared as a book,* Modern Architecture, *and two years
later—while celebrating his sixty-fifth birthday in 1932—he
published* The Disappearing City *and* An Autobiography. *That
same year, with the help and encouragement of his wife, he
founded the Taliesin Fellowship. These events brought him re-
newed publicity and by the mid-thirties he captured such seminal commissions as Fallingwater, the Johnson (Wax)
Administration Building, the Hanna house, and also unveiled
the first of his Usonian designs. With the fruits of these endeavors he built for himself a winter retreat near Phoenix, Arizona; he called it Taliesin West.*

*On the eve of the war he visited London to deliver four lec-
tures at the Royal Institute of British Architects as the Sir
George Watson Lecturer of the Sulgrave Manor Board; these
were published as* An Organic Architecture: the Architecture
of Democracy. *The British journals took great pleasure in de-*

Excerpts from, respectively, *The Architects' Journal* 89, May 11, 1939, p. 757,
and *Journal of the Royal Institute of British Architects* 46, May 22, 1939, p. 700.

scribing the architect from the long grass country of the

American Middle West.

By the time this journal appears the third of the four Sulgrave Manor sermons—for sermons they are, being concerned with architecture by way of nature and the art of living—will have been delivered by Frank Lloyd Wright at the R.I.B.A. At the evening meeting last Friday the audience overflowed into the aisles. The white-haired prophet was in form, disciples and disbelievers spellbound by his natural dignity, his obvious sincerity, his easy manner—or rather, his lack of anything so superficial as a manner. He has an irresistibly persuasive voice, mellow, smooth-flowing.

Frank Lloyd Wright is nothing if not American. But far from typically American, of course, if such a state of being exists. We are apt to forget, because of the tie of language, that Americans are "foreigners." Americans have an idiom not only in the expression of their speech but in the expression of their being. They have no taboos, for instance, about communicating what might be termed a nature-experience: they don't mind, most of them, admitting to a romantic reflex if they feel that way. We do. When Frank Lloyd Wright tells us he was born in the prairie, "out in the long grasses," we shift uneasily in our seats. When he talks of a building growing "out of the earth into the light" we get slightly clammy. But he gets away with it, for the good reason that he believes it and lives it. His lyrical philosophy, with its robust American tang, comes out full strength in his buildings. He remains the Walt Whitman of architecture. An individualist.

Mr. Frank Lloyd Wright's visit is over now, and the London architectural world, a bit dazed perhaps, is looking around to see how many of its old beliefs, or new ones, too, remain intact after the big bang. By the force of his personality, and the force of his provocative ideas, Mr. Lloyd Wright succeeded in making us stop and listen and think out quite a lot of things anew. It is too early to gauge how deep are the sympathies that have been made to exist between London modernism and Taliesin.

The whole argument has, as it were, been left in the air. The atmosphere of the meetings somehow was inimical to coherent and constructive discussion; probably there never can be really good discussion at meetings so large and so charged with feeling! Nevertheless, there were many there left with their doubts unresolved who, if circumstances had allowed, would easily enough have been satisfied.

Mr. Wright's critics and Mr. Wright seemed so easily to get at cross purposes, Mr. Wright presenting a formula, a general pattern of development, in a Marxian way, extending rationality in human problems to include spheres of life in which radical changes are all the time taking place; the critics all the time looking for an exactitude of solution which this extended reasoning could not allow. All along mystics have been asking such questions as "Please, Mr. Wright, where do I put the soil pipes in organic architecture?" and have had in reply answers which, to the people who put such questions, are certainly inadequate, and even frivolous, or seem dully of the "render unto Caesar" class of answer. But there is a lot more that can and will be said than ever has been said in the last few weeks, and certainly more than can be said in a paragraph here. Finally, however, once more a word of gratitude, not only to Mr. Wright, but also to the Sulgrave Manor Board, who made his visit possible.

With Wright at Taliesin West (1947)

Eric Mendelsohn

The war years led to a resurgence of American nationalism and inevitably caused a reassessment of cultural values. This brought Wright, in spite of his pacifist views, to the fore as a native son. Increasingly his name was linked to the tradition of Jefferson, Emerson, and Thoreau, and belatedly in 1942 the first English language book about his work appeared—Henry-Russell Hitchcock's In the Nature of Materials. *The architect was then seventy-five years old, and thirty-two years had passed since Wasmuth and others had begun publishing his work abroad—thus proving the old adage that genius goes without honor in his native land.*

San Francisco, 1947
At the solstice weekend we were at Frank Lloyd Wright's winter palace at Phoenix, Arizona, a thousand miles away from here [figures 19–20]. Such is the scale in this country! Wright will be seventy-nine this year. His resilience, vitality and creative power—both mental and physical—are phenomenal. He holds himself upright; his step is firm and springy; he has a sparkle of eternal youth. He speaks the way Emerson wrote; he overflows with an ebullience like that of Whitman in his clearest visions; he reflects on men, life and nature like Thoreau in his most serene observations.

Beyer, Oskar, ed. *Eric Mendelsohn: Letters of an Architect.* London, New York, and Toronto: Abelard-Schuman, 1967, pp. 158–159.

Taliesin West, his "Great Fugue." A desert, a carpet, a tented camp, prehistory and the twentieth century: a wave from the endless desert breaks on the shore of his own life. Human and superhuman, man and nature in organic unity—the touchstone for his own aims.

I have followed his work for thirty-five years. I was with him in 1924, 1941 and 1947 and we met often in the years between. My affection for him and my respect for his work remain unaltered. We are quite open, quite simple and direct with one another and are bound to one another by an inner affinity, both as men and as artists.

His singular greatness was more clearly apparent than ever this time; it has never been more evident than during the hours we spent on the lawn of his own patio, in front of his jewel of a living room—before us the flowering, ageless desert of Arizona.

He spoke of Sullivan, his "beloved master" and the latter's position in the development of contemporary architecture, and of his own work for and with him. Serious and dedicated, wise and knowledgeable, a true historian who has lived through his own history, a real philosopher . . . with all his hopes and disappointments, clearly aware of his limitations but with unlimited visions.

Every word rings true; no empty gesture; no play-acting. The sun itself and no sunspot. Wonderful days, most rare and unforgettable.

His last works signify the completion of all that for almost sixty years he has striven to resolve, to discover and to create, the sum of all the human drama, the dynamic will, the grandiose imagination and the creative abundance in him.

Outside the Profession (1953)

Anonymous

The decade following the war saw Wright become a national celebrity. He was interviewed on radio and television, quoted in the newspapers, and invited to lecture everywhere. His architectural practice flourished, yet each new design met with the same mixture of skepticism and scorn that had greeted his prairie houses, the Larkin Building, or Unity Temple nearly fifty years before. It is amazing that neither his creativity nor zeal seemed to slacken with advancing years.

The New Yorker, in its inimitable style, once again enjoyed an interview with Wright.

We've just had one of our annual talks with that merry, bitter, lively, ambitious, and beguiling man, Frank Lloyd Wright, who at eighty-four has more work under construction than ever before in his life. Wright is in town to get his plans for the Guggenheim Museum of Non-Objective Painting approved by our local building department—the museum has been about to be built for many a long year now, and Wright says patiently that he hopes ground will be broken for it next spring. . . .

We visited Mr. Wright in his suite high up in the Plaza. "I've stayed here on my visits for forty years," he said. "A beautiful

From an article in "The Talk of the Town" section in *The New Yorker* 29 September 26, 1953, pp. 26–27. Reprinted by permission, © 1953 The New Yorker Magazine, Inc.

hotel. They started to remodel it downstairs a few years back, but thank God I got here in time to stop them. The little devils had already wrecked the Palm Court, but I saved the Oak Room and the dining room." On a table between Wright and us were stout pots of tea, a plate of stout sandwiches, and a scattering of magazines and papers. As we talked, the table cloth was slowly darkened by an assortment of Wright graffiti, ranging from floor plans and elevations of houses, churches, and factories to a sketch of his Jaguar, which is currently his favorite car and is, he said, capable of reaching ninety without a tremor. Wright himself is so plainly capable of reaching ninety without a tremor that we couldn't help asking how he had managed to outwit age. At that moment, the telephone rang, and he bounded to his feet to answer it. "Damned thing rings all day!" he said with pleasure. Over the telephone, he made an appointment for nine the next morning, and then re-turned to his tea. "I have seven children and ten grandchildren and three great-grandchildren, so I must be old, but I don't feel old, I feel young," he said. "I draw and build and teach my apprentices and send them out into the world, not to be like me but to be themselves. At last count, a hundred and sixty-eight practicing architects had been trained by me at Taliesin, in Wisconsin. When can I ever have been readier to do good work? When can I ever have been fitter to be alive, to help build an American culture? Not a civilization, because we al-ready have a civilization, but a culture. And you can't have a culture without an architecture."

The telephone rang again, and Wright, racing to it, exclaimed, "*Damn* the thing!" He made an appointment for ten the next morning, hung up, ruffled his bright-blue flowing tie, took a deep breath, and asked us please not to consider him a mem-ber of the architectural profession. "I'm not a member of any profession," he said. "I'm a one-man experiment in democ-racy, an experiment that worked. An individual who rose by his own merits, beholden to no one. When Sullivan and I came to architecture, it had been slumbering for five hundred years. We woke it up. We gave it a fresh start. We made it organic. We said architecture was space to be lived in, not a facade, not a box, not a monument. Wallie Harrison says the slab's the thing. I say the cemeteries are full of slabs, but who wants to be in a cemetery? Does all this sound arrogant? Let it sound arrogant, then!" . . .

We could see that Wright was, if anything, freshening as he went along, but we felt our own strength ebbing, and between telephone calls for him (a date for eleven the next morning, a date for an early lunch) we hastened to ask about his latest work. "I've designed a white marble building to be built in Venice, right on the Grand Canal," he said. "The first new building to go up there since heaven knows when. It's to be a memorial to a young Italian architect who was killed in an accident in this country, and aside from the Imperial Hotel in Tokyo, it's the only work I've designed for anywhere outside the United States. I've always felt that the rest of the world was entitled to its own kinds of culture. Then, I've designed a new bridge for San Francisco. They're holding a referendum out there to see whether they want to put it up or not. And a housing project for Madison, Wisconsin. They're holding a referendum on that, too. And a skyscraper for Bartlesville, Oklahoma. A beautiful thing in its own park. I designed it first for New York, thirty years ago. It was going to be built down in the Bowery. By now, I'm used to waiting for my buildings to come true. Six hundred and forty of them have come true so far. I've never had a building in New York. This is my first." He jumped up and peered out the window, to where Fifth Avenue glittered and shook with the roofs of cars. "I'm flying home to Taliesin tomorrow afternoon," he said. "We have thirty-five hundred acres out there. My family followed the Indians onto that land. The name of our town is Spring Green." He said the name twice over—"Spring Green. Spring Green"—then burst out happily, "Out there, chickens give eggs, cows give milk, and old Wright he rides his Tennessee walking horse."

My Husband . . . (1966)

Olgivanna Lloyd Wright

*Told by the person closest to him of all—these are the recol-
lections of his wife. Married late in the twenties, they shared
life for over thirty years. Together they experienced the full
course of Wright's "second" career—beginning in the lean
twenties and early thirties, continuing through the founding of
the Taliesin Fellowship in 1932, and culminating in the many
splendid architectural achievements prior to Wright's death in
1959.*

*Nowhere will one find a more penetrating explanation than
this of how Wright thought, worked, and reacted to the world
around him.*

He loved the mornings of his life best, the times that were
marked with the most productive activity, and liked to be
stimulated then by opposing thoughts which could stir him to
produce still more varied forms.

He never took anything for granted. An idea which might have
originated from some remote source, even a political talk we
might have discussed, would eventually present itself in the
form of a drawing to him. It was not necessarily the thought

Wright, Olgivanna Lloyd. *Frank Lloyd Wright, His Life, His Work, His Words.* New
York: Horizon Press, 1966, pp. 86, 87, 88, 170, 169, 179, 112, 135, 140, 141, 145,
174, 175, 178.

itself, but the energy produced by it that worked on him; he did his work in designing with a power that was unceasing.

When he had given concrete form to a concept in his mind, he would immediately put it down on the drafting board. Usually the students would stand over him and watch him design, and after he had finished his drawing he would sit down, in turn, at each student's drafting table to see what he was doing, making suggestions, indicating necessary changes.

The human element was more important to him than architectural talent and what he appreciated most in a student was a sense of personal responsibility.

He would take endless time with a seventeen-year-old, talking to him as though he were a man of forty, placing complete responsibility on the youth's shoulders for executing his work, always with the aim of raising himself in his own estimation as a creative individual capable of facing himself, his society, and his Creator without fear. Because he considered that the most important thing to teach youth is love of their work, he felt they should be helped in making sure to choose work they loved; and from that basis everything else, including marriage, would then take place proportionately.

Nothing pleased him more than to receive letters from thirteen- or fourteen-year-olds asking him how they should pursue the architectural profession. He always answered them. Between him and youth there was a spontaneous, natural bond; he spoke to them with love, understanding their plight as if he saw their future clearly and wanted to prepare them for it, not in a pragmatic, material sense, but in a creative sense, for the sustenance of their spirit. Perhaps they were to him a reflection of himself, for in his early years he was always in search of a better life.

In talking to him you had a sense of his complete poise, as though in some way nothing ever disturbed him, no sorrow touched him, though much sorrow marked his life.

He believed the role of an architect to be that of a builder, not only of buildings but of the social structure, because he felt that if society were given conditions in which buildings had intelligence and raison d'être the whole structure of human society itself would have the substance of strength and

The Man: His Personality and Life-Style

beauty. Interested in politics and affairs of state, he believed that architecture as the plan-in-structure of all things was the all-inclusive basis for every civilization and culture. So he repeatedly related architecture to democracy, considering democracy the highest form of aristocracy man has ever known, a society based on the sovereignty of the individual.

My husband would listen insatiably to music for hours at a time. Loud-speakers, concealed in various places aroung Taliesin, played for five or six hours during the day, until everybody begged me to have them turned off. To him a building, too, sang: architecture was a harmony of planes, depths and heights, the spirit of life, "the expression of man," and so he spoke in terms of the structural quality of a musical composition. He believed that, in an inner sense, music and architecture are one.

He loved books. He loved William Blake, Walt Whitman, Emerson, Thoreau, and valued Samuel Butler in *The Way of All Flesh*, which he thought faithfully represented its era. In such novels, he thought, history was better recorded than in orthodox historical works. He often spoke of Tolstoy as the best representative of his time and especially admired *War and Peace* and *Resurrection*. He appreciated Dostoevsky who, he thought, had best interpreted the search and indecision of those immersed in the wild passions and sorrows of the spirit that characterized his age. Dickens too he enjoyed.

Among the French novelists he read avidly were Victor Hugo, whom he often quoted, and Dumas, particularly his *The Three Musketeers*.

Of the American writers to whom he introduced me, among his best-loved humorists were Mark Twain, O. Henry, and Thurber, whose stories he liked to read aloud to me. He was always reading to me or I to him and we had many a hilarious evening laughing together. It was in *The Four Million* that he thought O. Henry best reflected his times, touched with sadness, a mixture of tenderness and tragedy.

When he was preoccupied in a book, he would vanish altogether, and when he emerged he referred constantly to the book he was reading, often identifying completely with its author and his creative process.

He cared little for the modern novels, especially the best-sellers, which disappear as fast as they are published. Magazines, journals, newspapers, he devoured at terrific speed, particularly when we traveled, but the work of great writers he read with slow contemplation. Literature occupied a high level in his life; but he did not connect it, like music, with architecture. "Literature tells about man," he often said, "architecture presents him."

The highest expression of culture to him meant translating great ideas into action. I believe it was because of his faith in that ideal that he had such an acute interest in philosophy, literature, and poetry. It prompted him to open every book with curiosity in order to find something which could be utilized for the best in himself. He believed that reading books on philosophy was most important, a point on which we met from the very beginning of our life together. It was the inner structure of life that he explored first and only then moved into exterior form.

Philosophy as he saw it was in the abstract. No matter how abstract its expression, he utilized it in some imaginative way in his work. His architecture bears the image of thought and feeling and is eternally alive. When we enter a building of his, we sense at once a fourth-dimensional quality beyond its three-dimensional aspect, some mystery in it that everyone, according to his ability, receives.

He often said that beauty was the highest form of morality and sought it wherever he was, in whatever he did. The idea of organic architecture was the flesh and blood of his being. He saw the universe through architecture. He saw it in the structure of all nature, and often referred to his work as harmonious or intrinsic, an architecture of inner harmony with the exterior world. He truly believed that a beautiful building can help man dissolve the conflicts in his life, that a harmonious building has a quieting effect upon us and serves us as inspiration. Even those who speak of improving surroundings often forget that it is architecture, in its influence on the human psyche, that is the most important of all.

His intimacy with nature enabled him to translate it into architectural terms. In the patterns of nature, the formation of a snowflake, a mountain, a crystal, a field, an ocean, a running brook, the indentations and lines in a jagged rock hanging over the sea, it was an inner beat, an inner rhythm he listened to, the inner character that he transferred to paper without copying or imitating any form, bringing never-ending variety into architecture. No blade of grass is a replica of another any more than a mountain is identical to another, and he grasped this individuality not only in his mind but through something much more complex; some call it extrasensory perception or intuitive sense or instinct, but it was beyond even these, a genius, cut in a different pattern from other men, that has appeared rarely in our history.

Frank Lloyd Wright's Funeral (April 12, 1959)

John Noble Richards

Wright's final years witnessed the creation of such imaginative

projects as the Arizona State Capitol, Marin County Govern-

ment Center, Bagdad Opera House, Annunciation Greek Or-

thodox Church, Mile High—not to mention innumerable

house designs. Seemingly there was no end to the creative

and controversial ideas that sprang from his lively mind

until—shortly before his ninety-second birthday and following

minor surgery—Wright took a long, deep breath and died.

It was a bright and chilly Sunday afternoon.
Taliesin East appeared saddened, the smoke
from its massive chimneys curling lazily
up to the sky, as the famous house
looked out over and guarded the Wisconsin valley.

Two beautiful horses stood resting in the courtyard,
hitched to a little red dray, which was to carry
Frank Lloyd Wright to the chapel
and his final resting place.

Friends and neighbors gathered,
shortly before five o'clock,
at the old chapel, which is located
on a dirt road about three-quarters of a mile
from the entrance to Taliesin East.
They assembled quietly and talked in hushed voices.

Journal of the American Institute of Architects 31, May 1959, p. 44.
Reproduced with the permission of the AIA Journal, copyright 1959, The American Institute of Architects.

The walls and roof of the chapel
are covered with weather-beaten shingles,
mellowed to a warm gray. It nestles
in a grove of tall and stately pine trees,
which seemed to give forth a saddened tune
as they moved in the late afternoon breeze.

The old cemetery adjacent to the chapel
on the east and the south, is the burial ground
of many of Frank Lloyd Wright's relatives. His
mother's grave lies directly to the south of his.
Old tombstones bear the names of Lloyd, Jones
and Wright. The area immediately surrounding his
grave was covered with pine boughs, yellow
chrysanthemums, and bird of paradise flowers
mingling with the boughs.

The interior of the chapel is extremely simple
and plain. It was decorated with pine boughs
on either side of the platform. Large candelabra
with yellow candles flickered in the twilight.
The chapel seats about a hundred and fifty in its
low plywood pews. The odor of the pine, the candles
and the new wood of the pews was pleasant and
relaxing. It is heated by a small pot-bellied stove,
which was kept going with some difficulty.

The chapel bell, pulled by a rope at the rear, started
to toll about five o'clock. Some
of the friends gathered there,
left their seats and stood outside
between the road and the chapel.

The funeral procession was now visible
as it came down the hill from Taliesin East.
The little red dray, drawn by the two horses
and driven by two of his students, carried
Mr. Wright's casket. It was covered
by a rose-colored fabric
and a single pine bough.

Mrs. Wright, members of the family and friends
followed the catafalque, walking
behind it, as the procession moved slowly

down the hill toward the highway. The horses
seemed to sense their responsibility
as they moved slowly along the road.

Turning off the highway and on to the dirt road,
the procession moved to the entrance gate
of the chapel. Friends lined the east side
of the walk as Frank Lloyd Wright was carried
up the steps, into the chapel, and placed
on the platform.

The minister of the First Unitarian Church
of Madison waited until all was quiet
before he spoke. His message was simple
and thoughtful, and he read portions
of the Bible which mention truth and genius.

The six tall bearers of the casket carried
Frank Lloyd Wright's remains to the cemetery.
As the casket was lowered into
the grave, one of his students read from
Wright's autobiography. As it
was read, Mrs. Wright repeated the lines,
to herself, with the reader.
The minister read the final words.

The pine trees swayed gently
in the twilight, as the relatives, friends
and associates of the great man moved slowly
away from the chapel toward their homes.

His place in history is secure.
His continuing influence assured.
This century's architectural achievements
would be unthinkable without him.
He has been a teacher to all of us.

Part II

Wright's Clients and His Work

Any discussion of Wright would be incomplete without some commentary from his clients, especially since his buildings provide for so much more than just their basic needs. He created an environment for living that administers to their mental health and adds greater richness and enjoyment to their lives. To accomplish this a house must teach, as well as serve, and for this reason even a casual visitor is struck by the strong, firm, but always gentle and restful, character of a Wright-designed house.

The texts that follow discuss Wright's attitude toward his clients, the give-and-take between architect and client during the process of design, and the reaction that people have to living in a Wright house. And, finally, comments by co-workers provide insights as to how he designed and built these splendid homes.

An Original-Owner Interview Survey of Frank Lloyd Wright's Residential Architecture (1972)

Eugene R. Streich

Wright's attitude toward his clients, as well as the remarkable quality of life that his homes provide, is corroborated by an in-depth survey conducted by human-factors scientist Eugene R. Streich. Having interviewed thirty-three original owners, and using 159 questions as the core of his survey, Streich compiled the data from which the following paper was prepared.

Researchers interested in our psychological health and well-being are most welcome to the field of Wright studies. Wright was, in fact, one of the great psychologists of our time. He not only comprehended our needs, and the little everyday experiences that enhance the quality of our lives, but he knew how these could be provided for. Therein much of his genius lies.

Streich's findings dispel many false beliefs about Wright, especially the distorted notion of some that he cared little for the special needs of clients. It is revealing, in this context, to note

Mitchell, William J., ed. *Environmental Design, Research and Practice: Proceedings of the EDRA 3/AR8 Conference, University of California at Los Angeles, January 1972*, Volume II, pp. 13–10–1 to 13–10–8.
Reprinted by permission, William J. Mitchell.

Streich's reason for undertaking such a survey: ". . .the actual

impetus for the study resulted from a weekend visit to

Wright's home in Wisconsin in 1956. The writer, observing a

two-hour design critique by Wright of his students' work, was

struck by the fact that Wright's entire critique was based upon

user considerations rather than the usual (and expected) em-

phasis upon form, proportion, scale, or other visual elements.

At that time the writer began to speculate about what the ac-

tual users of Wright's houses might report."

Introduction

Although he created an extraordinary range of architectural designs, Frank Lloyd Wright can be considered as primarily a residential architect. Approximately 70 per cent of his total output of separate and distinct building designs were single-family residential. The percentage is even higher when one compares those designs actually built with unexecuted projects. Further, this ratio of residential to non-residential designs remained remarkably consistent throughout his professional career. The actual count is as follows:

Residential	653
Non-residential	276
Total	929

The Problem

Most members of the design profession are familiar with Wright's residential work as a considerable portion has been extensively published. However, not much is known about: (1) the interaction between Wright and his clients during the design phase, and (2) once built and occupied, how his houses "worked" as design solutions.

It was the primary purpose of this study to obtain information concerning these two aspects of Wright's work by going directly to the persons involved—the clients. A secondary, long-range, objective was that, hopefully, the data would provide a partial basis for the development of an evaluation framework (or scale) with which to measure the "quality" of a residential design.

Method

In order to maintain consistency throughout the survey, a set of 159 questions was developed and formed the basis for interviews with the client-owners. There were eight categories of questions:

	Number of Questions
Origin of commission: Why Wright?	11
Nature of owner's original requirements	23
Initial contact with Wright and extent of interaction during the planning phase	18
Construction/supervision experiences	16
How did the house "work"?	54
Maintenance practices and problems	17
Later modifications and/or additions	15
In retrospect: Owners' overall impressions	5
Total	159

In addition to obtaining information from owners, a number of other sources were used in the study, primarily to verify ambiguous points:

Two visits to Taliesin, Wright's home in Wisconsin, were made to examine the files. A review of working drawings, particularly in those instances where alternate design schemes had been prepared, provided an opportunity to trace design modifications through their various stages.

Several discussions with John Howe, the head of the drafting office during Wright's later years, provided insight into the operation of Wright's studio.

At the time of the owner interviews it became possible to interview five of the building contractors involved. Questions concerning adequacy of working drawings, supervision, and construction costs were clarified.

Findings: General Comments

As a result of conducting this survey, the writer has learned to distrust the *entire* body of folklore that has grown up around Wright's architecture. Most, if not all, of it is just not true. For example:

"Only wealthy clients could afford Wright." Actually, most of his clients were of quite modest means. There were scarcely ten really wealthy clients in his sixty-five years of residential practice.

"Wright arrogantly dictates the design to his clients." The evidence is to the contrary. Wright invariably conducted all discussions with his clients personally and took considerable pains to ascertain the client's requirements and living habits. However, when Wright felt a client was ill informed in requesting a particular feature, he could be extraordinarily persuasive. He was also persuasive when he personally favored a particular design scheme for a given site.

"Wright was lax in supervision of construction." Again, not true in the sense intended. The only reports of his early work are those of clients Angster, Boynton, Greene, and Robie, who pointedly indicate a remarkable attention to detail on Wright's part. In later years, when his residential practice was (literally) nationwide, the picture is less clear. Wright himself, as an elderly man (and an increasingly busy one), visited construction sites less frequently as the years went on. Field supervision was delegated to his senior staff apprentices who either periodically traveled to, or resided [at] the site. Problems did arise, but were usually resolved without much delay. The Kaufmann house, "Fallingwater," is an example.

"Wright's roofs leaked." A few (very few) did. There were other problems too, but probably no more than occur in the practice of any architectural firm doing innovative work.

Specific Findings

Space limitations in this paper do not permit reporting findings on each individual residence in the study. Instead, summary information is provided in the following numbered categories:

Type of Clientele   Wright's residential clients, with very few exceptions, belonged to the upper-middle socio-economic level. A considerable percentage were salaried members of various professions such as college professors, high school teachers, librarians and research chemists. Others, non-salaried, were lawyers, doctors, and small businessmen, including several contractors and the owner of a gas station. Their educational level was probably higher than average. Typically, at least one member of the family had a strong interest in the arts. It is probably safe to say that they were somewhat more independent-minded than the average person.

Choice of Wright as Architect In most cases, the decision to approach Wright to be their architect was made by husband and wife jointly. It was usually the result of considerable study of publications on his work, and lengthy family discussions. Sometimes, a single member of the family (usually the wife) was the active force in the choice. There were two instances where college age children, upon learning their parents were planning to build, were instrumental in Wright's being selected. Occasionally, a client liked a particular published, but unexecuted, design and contacted Wright about having it built (the Walter house). One owner admitted to an initial acquisitive motive. "I wanted one of the old boy's masterpieces before he died. I figured it couldn't help but go up in value after his death—like an art work. But now that I have lived in it, I like it and wouldn't sell it for anything."

Wright's Acceptance of the Commission Apparently, most clients approached Wright with some trepidation. "We really didn't think someone of his stature would bother with us" was a typically expressed feeling. In this sample, of course, all clients had been accepted, although many of them were so notified by mail after an initial face-to-face discussion. As an amusing aside, John Howe, the former head of Wright's drafting studio, reports that: "Wright developed a high regard for his clients simply because they were *his* clients. He found virtues in them which were indiscernible to others and almost refused to acknowledge their shortcomings."

Architect/Client Interaction After approaching Wright to be their architect, the clients were invited to visit Wright at one of the two Taliesins. Along with the invitation, they were provided with a brochure setting forth the fee arrangements: "Ten percent of the cost of the completed building which invariably includes the planting of the grounds and the major furnishings considered as part of the building scheme." They were requested to provide an accurate topographical survey of the property, as complete a list of requirements as possible, and cautioned that "Dwelling-houses upon urban lots will not be accepted. Acreage is indispensable." (The latter admonishment was apparently not always adhered to, as a number of the residences were found to be on suburban lots.)

Almost all owners reported that, to their surprise, Wright proved to be remarkably easy to get along with in negotiations over the design. There were a number of instances where Wright either extensively modified a design or created one or more new schemes. In some cases where cost was a factor, Wright's staff dimensionally scaled down the design, while keeping the original concept intact.

Wright's Use of a Design Grid   Wright consistently used a geometric grid (rectangles, triangles, diamonds, hexagonals, etc.) as a basis for developing his floor plan. Not always apparent was his use of a concomitant vertical unit system based upon masonry courses or boards and battens. This practice proved to be a mixed blessing for contractors. Laying out the grid was a precise and demanding task. However, once construction was underway, workmen were able to locate their finish work directly to lines on the floor slab and to vertical courses.

Typical Residential Configuration   The residences in the sample followed Wright's usual "polliwog" configuration: The "body" being the living and social area (living room, dining area and kitchen) with the "tail" containing bedrooms and bath. Almost all of Wright's later residential designs are variations on this basic theme.

Construction/Superintendence   The construction phase posed problems for almost all the owners. Sometimes the search for a sympathetic and competent contractor was difficult. Wright's foundation specifications and some of his roof support arrangements were considered dubious by authorities, delaying or denying the issuance of building permits. Mortgage sources were few and far between. Wright's organization helped where possible with advice on bids, or costs for special millwork. A senior staff apprentice was designated to superintend construction at the site.

Do-it-Yourself Instances   The Berger, Grant and Lovness residences were built from the ground up by the owners. All three were well executed. The writer knows of two others which were partially owner-built (and look it). One in particular is atrociously executed.

Another version of do-it-yourselfism developed among a group of Upjohn Institute chemists in Kalamazoo, Michigan. Seeking good housing at low cost, they formed a non-profit organization. They obtained the services of Wright to lay out the master site plan and design some of the houses, brought masonry and lumber by the trainload, and then helped each other over the rough spots of construction. Portions of the work on these houses was performed by contractors.

Siting   Comments on the way the house was sited on the property were unanimously enthusiastic. Apparently, this was one area where Wright's talent was unequivocally demonstrated.

"Rock Ballast" Foundations   Contractors reported that Wright's use of crushed rock instead of standard footings saved about 20% on foundation costs. No problems were reported, although some owners expressed concern over possible future difficulties with heating pipes beneath the slab.

Basements   Wright did not favor basements and strongly advised clients against them. Nevertheless, a few partial basements were included at client insistence.

Handling of Masonry   Wright used several masonry treatments which provided attractive visual effects, but were expensive. For red brick walls he specified red cement for all vertical joints and white cement for the horizontal joints. (This required the masons to use two mortar boards.) In cement block walls he favored setting every other course out (or in) one-half inch to create a shadow line. Again, a costly procedure, particularly where other work had to join to the masonry.

Fireplaces   Almost all owners report gratification with their fireplace(s), both as to location and function. There was a period in the late nineteen thirties, however, when Wright had a tendency to stretch the height of the fireplace opening to its functional limit. The fireplaces in the Willey, Johnson, and Manson houses are examples. The Manson fireplace smoked sufficiently to necessitate an inspection trip by Wright and several apprentices. Wright and company promptly reduced the height of the opening by adding several courses of brick.

Ventilation Reyner Banham [see p. 155] has reported on the surprisingly advanced environmental control features in two of Wright's early works, the Robie and Baker houses. Wright has continued these same practices now somewhat modified, by creating a raised ceiling over the kitchen with clerestory windows for ventilation. Thus the kitchen space becomes the venting flue for the social portion of the house. As one owner remarked: "Best damn cocktail party house in the neighborhood. You open those vents and all the smoke drifts to the kitchen and disappears."

Heating Wright's later houses were typically heated by hot water circulating in pipes beneath the slab. This furnished satisfactory heat in mild climates, and in northern areas as long as only throw rugs were used. However, when wall-to-wall carpeting was laid, as it was in several houses, substantial heat loss occurred. Eventually supplemental baseboard heating was added in these homes.

Kitchens The largest bone of contention among clients' wives was the kitchen. The complaints were many and varied: "It's too small." "I can't look out and watch the children." (Wright kitchens were usually centrally located, skylighted, and without windows.) "When I drop things on the concrete slab they break."

On the other hand, two design features were universally acclaimed: (1) Wright used a mix of open and closed shelves such that items in daily use were readily at hand while less frequently used items could be stored out of sight. (2) Wright very skillfully so positioned the kitchen in relation to the dining and living room areas that a housewife could make herself part of a social group or isolate herself by choosing a particular part of the kitchen in which to work.

Bathrooms Wright "family" bathrooms were typically compact and usually located between a pair of bedrooms in the "tail" of the house. Occasionally a powder room would be ingeniously located just off the living room area and would elicit appreciative comment from guests.

Bedrooms Like the bathrooms, the bedrooms were treated in utilitarian fashion and are probably the least "Wrightian" features in most of the residences, particularly those in the lower cost range. Even when space was restricted, however, Wright found ways to incorporate a small built-in writing table in a corner, or a reading alcove.

"Working" Hallways   In one form or another, each of the residences incorporated Wright's concept of using a hallway for several purposes. Typically a corridor would include a bank of storage cabinets or bookshelves along its entire length, sometimes broken up with a bench or shelf, and usually receiving light from a series of windows above the cabinets. Owners liked this feature for several reasons. It "organized" the storage and put it away from the social side of the house. It also added a touch of visual excitement to an otherwise utilitarian element.

Internal "Vistas"   One of the recognized features of a Wright residence is the presence of one or more visually delightful internal "vistas" equal to those looking toward outside views. A number of his larger residences were noted for these features (the Coonley and Johnson houses). Occasionally Wright was able to incorporate this feature in a smaller residence [as, for example, when] a person in the living room can observe a fire burning in a bedroom fireplace at the end of a long hallway.

Maintenance Considerations   Some of Wright's early residences have not held up well, particularly those with board and plaster exteriors, and some extended cantilevers have shown deformation. In contrast, his later residences have required remarkably little maintenance, primarily due to the use of identical materials inside and out. Where possible, Wright specified integral coloring in his cement and plaster surfaces. Cracks are evident in plastered soffits in many instances where, according to clients, economy measures were employed during construction.

Modifications and/or Additions   Most residences in the sample remain substantially as designed and constructed. A few were planned for later expansion (the Berger, Brown, Hanna, and Kaufmann residences). The previously mentioned Berger residence was designed, at the client's request, as a three-stage do-it-yourself project.

Other owners (Oboler and Stevens) went back to Wright repeatedly for design alterations and additions due to changes in their family configurations. It was interesting to observe that most clients would think twice about altering any of Wright's work, while Wright himself apparently did not view it as all that sacred. When requested, he would cheerfully undertake anything from minor alterations to drastic residential surgery.

Non-Surviving Residences   It is worth noting that the Fuller residence designed in 1951 and located at Pass Christian, Mississippi was demolished by Hurricane Camille in 1969. Several others have been damaged by fire.

The Question of Cost   Were Wright's residences costly to build? A number of his houses were *very* large and *very* expensive (the Avery Cooney, Darwin Martin and Herbert Johnson houses). Several smaller houses could be considered expensive for their size (the Neils, Kaufmann and Walter houses). All three required complex construction techniques, and the latter two were built in remote areas. However, most of Wright's residences were probably no more expensive than comparable-sized dwellings of other custom designers. A few clients, willing to do some or all of the construction work, came through with remarkably low expense.

The Unexecuted Designs   A major question remains unanswered. Approximately 55% of Wright's residential designs were never built. The percentage is surprisingly high. Why? This study discovered a high level of owner satisfaction for built designs. Those clients who could not, or chose not to, build may present a different story and deserve a separate investigation.

Summary
If you are the original owner of a Frank Lloyd Wright house, you typically

are in the upper middle socio-economic level;

are probably somewhat better educated (or at least more well read) than others in your level;

have a streak of independence in your makeup;

deliberated a long time before approaching Wright, and then with some trepidation;

were pleasantly surprised at how attentive and agreeable Wright was in preliminary discussions;

waited a considerable length of time for the preliminary sketches to arrive;

if anything, waited even longer for the working drawings;

searched far afield for a contractor who was (1) willing, and (2) reasonable;

received a jolt when the construction bids began coming in;

in some instances, returned to Wright to see what could be done to cut costs;

again, were pleasantly surprised to find Wright willing to modify the design (downward) and/or substitute other materials (cheaper);

stood by observing, with pride, when the ground was broken;

stood by later, aghast, as workmen took frequent and unconscionably long periods of time to study the blueprints;

vowed, toward the end of construction, that you would never do it again;

moved in and spent the next year or two discovering a series of unexpected delights (and a few quirky features);

found your life somewhat altered, in subtle ways, ever since;

sooner or later found reasons to throw out some of the Wright-designed furniture;

eventually became resigned to dealing with a seemingly unending stream of visitors.

Mr. Robie Knew What He Wanted (1907/1958)

Frederick C. Robie

*Built near the campus of the University of Chicago between
1907 and 1909, the Robie house stands as the classic example
of a prairie house (figures 11–12). The client, Frederick C. Robie, was a prosperous young bicycle manufacturer who in
1958 was interviewed by his son.*

*Father, one thing many people have been interested in for the
past forty years is what kind of house did you want in the first
place?*

I definitely wanted it fireproof, and unlike the sort of thing
prevalent in the homes of that period. The idea of most of
those houses was a kind of conglomeration of architecture, on
the outside, and they were absolutely cut up inside. I wanted
sunlight in my living room in the morning before I went to
work, and I wanted to be able to look out and down the street
to my neighbors without having them invade my privacy. I certainly didn't want a lot of junk—a lot of fabrics, draperies, and
what not, or old-fashioned roller shades with the brass fittings
on the ends—in my line of vision, gathering dust and interfer-
ing with window washing. No sir. I didn't want any wide trim
on the doorways or windows. I wanted it narrow, to bring in a
wider window, to give me more light.

I wanted to have the bedroom quarters and nursery activities
separate and exclusively for the use of the children, all this to
be offset on the side by a master bedroom, with a fireplace. I
wanted a brick wall to keep the children from wandering out of

Architectural Forum 109, October 1958, pp. 126–127, 206, 210 the yard and getting lost. The whole thing was so nebulous that I could not explain it to anybody.

How about architects?

I probably contacted indirectly or directly a half dozen of these men. I did a little traveling around, and ran across a constant fillip: "I know what you want, one of those damn Wright houses." It was a good advertisement for Mr. Wright. I contacted him, and from the first we had a definite community of thought. When I talked in mechanical terms, he talked and thought in architectural terms. I thought, well, he was in my world.

Father, what year was that?

That was, let's see, that was long about Christmastime, 1906. We agreed on a procedure. He would make sketches and submit them within a reasonable time. I told him flat I didn't expect to build immediately. Take his time—which he did, and *how*. He spent a great deal of energy and thought and time, and he became more enthusiastic about the possibilities as he was able to work out the puzzle of placing rooms.

He had some commitment on hand, but we were not in a hurry. We were very comfortable, happy, and the difference of a few months would mean nothing in our lifetime. Here was a structure that was going to last as long as we lived, we hoped. And it was going to be a comfortable place.

Did you have any trouble in getting building permits owing to the house's unusual construction?

In purchasing the plot, I was under a verbal obligation to build a house which would cost a minimum of about $20,000. That was well within the figure I had in mind. In about a year, we decided that we'd go ahead. By then Mr. Wright and I were in hearty accord. Practically the last detail that I, as future occupant and owner, had to attend to was to be sure that all the contracts were signed, and so on, and funds made available to the contractor who was to pay the bill. It only took probably a couple of hours, but it took a lot of thought, and I wanted to conserve my investments until the funds were probably going to be needed.

During this period, Mr. Wright had done a beautiful job of weeding out the contractors. He covered the bids with meticulous care. I was amazed. The man who finally built the house was a man by the name of Barnard & Co. He was a go-getting, two-fisted, high-spitting sort of guy, and was a thorough mechanic in the art of household construction, having been in it from the day he was about sixteen. At his first job, I believe, he carried the beer to the contractor's men.

Once we began, progress went very rapidly. With practically no delay he put in the chimney, and the side walls then went up carefully. Every two or three layers of brick, in order to preserve the continuity and the long-line appearance, Mr. Barnard checked it with an instrument. There wasn't any by-guess-or-by-God business. He did a beautiful job; it developed into what I wanted, and what was satisfactory to Mr. Wright. The architect was responsible for that, and he took his responsibility very seriously. I know he was often on the job bright and early in the morning and stayed as long as he and Mr. Barnard wanted to settle things. The plans were so perfect that Barnard afterward told me he might as well have been making a piece of machinery.

It wasn't long before we were under cover. I went away on a business trip and came back and found the roof on, the walls up, and they were getting ready to cover the concrete floors with wood. And a beautiful job they did of that. Of course you could get wood in those days that is pretty difficult to get today.

There was some experimentation in the house: the building of indirect lighting around the side walls of the living room, for example, and the introduction of indirect heating by having the radiators strung along in the floor in front of doorways and windows with the pipes actually below the floor, which helped warm up the slabs, so that there was no shock of stepping on the cold floor, particularly in the bedrooms.

Relationships with Mr. Wright were ideal. It seems inconceivable that the foresight, the knowledge, and the intense desire to do just the right thing could have been embedded in a man like him—possibly it was in his hair—remember, it was kind of long.

Were there any extras on the job?

None. The actual total cost of the house proper, including all items—even interest and taxes, was $35,000. The cost of the lot was $14,000. Special furnishings, such as a hand-woven rug from Austria, which was provided under Mr. Wright's direction, came to about $10,000.

So your total cost was about?

$59,000.

And the budget you had set up in your own mind was what?

$60,000. It was one of the cleanest business deals I ever had.

The Love Affair of a Man and His House
(1939/1948)

Loren Pope

This is perhaps the most moving tribute ever paid to a Frank Lloyd Wright house. It is written with sensitivity and charm. Speaking of his house, the author says "It is like living with a great and quiet soul . . . its peace and calm carry over to you . . . it does not intrude, but is always there to comfort." The writer appreciates how architecture can affect the in-dweller; surely if more people were aware of this we might have a better world in which to live.

In publishing this article the editors were apprehensive. They prefaced it by saying "This story of what a modern house means to its owners came to House Beautiful *unsolicited. We held it for more than a year before we decided to be brave enough to publish it. We say "brave" because it will make a lot of our readers very angry. But since it is true that a house is so much more than mere shelter, we think people ought to know about it."*

House Beautiful 90, August 1948, pp. 32–34, 80, 90.
Reprinted by permission from *House Beautiful Magazine*, copyright 1948, The Hearst Corporation. All rights reserved.

How sad. How sad to think that the truth about architecture cannot be told—because it might make people "angry." How sad to think that architecture, for most people, is nothing more than shelter: an anonymous shell decorated according to prevailing taste.

The Loren Pope house (1939) is one of Wright's first Usonian homes, the earliest being his Jacobs house of 1937. These houses brilliantly infuse the spatial planning of the prairie house in a smaller, less costly structure, thus achieving a sense of interior spaciousness, and restfulness, which the actual dimensions seem to deny. The house itself nestles close to the ground, set on a concrete slab that contains the radiant heating. The Usonian house represents one of Wright's greatest achievements and points the way to future spatial solutions as our residences, of necessity, are becoming ever smaller (see figures 25–26).

For six years we lived in a truly modern house, designed and built for us by Frank Lloyd Wright, [and] we want to tell what it has meant to us.

[What we have found is] it is the only kind of habitation fit for man because it has a presence and a soul. Why? First, because it is a work of principle. And the other reasons grow out of the first. Because it is a work of principle, it is honest, and being honest, it is both eloquent and quiet. Buildings are close to our lives and influence them, consciously or subconsciously. Mr. Wright's buildings are a tangible expression of his philosophy. He thinks of America as synonymous with freedom. And to him, freedom has many ingredients; among them truth, courage, frankness, and space to live in, uncramped. All these things are a part of the house and proclaim themselves, eloquently but quietly.

Thus, the material that does the work also furnishes the decoration with its own charm. The house is free and open and gives a sense of space and release a free man responds to. The outdoors is so adroitly made a part of the living scheme that the dweller breathes as deeply as in a meadow in spring. And he obtains the same kind of unburdening of the little worries of life. That may sound fantastic to one who has never experienced it, but it is true. It is like living with a great and quiet soul. Some of its peace and calm carry over to you. That is one reason I say it is the only kind of house fit for man to live in. It is a lift for his soul as well as shelter for his body. It is an implicit sermon on truth, beauty, and simplicity. It does not intrude, but is always there for comfort.

As for the evidence, we might as well begin at the beginning, because it offers some.

We don't think anyone ever built a house with more warnings in their ears than we did. We heard tales about how much more Wright's buildings cost than he figured; how little he cared about his clients' means or their wishes; and how we would find ourselves with a white elephant on our hands.

There were other fantastic falsities. But we were aware that a man isn't shot at unless he towers too high above the herd. We also were aware that none of the architects we were acquainted with had ever claimed to have built a house within five hundred dollars of his estimate of the cost.

But because we had faith in the principles and in their enunciator and practitioner, we set no cost limit on Mr. Wright. We told him what kind of house we wanted, and that our income was on the shady side of $3,000 a year. We knew that our trust would not be betrayed, and it wasn't—despite the unusual hazards we were facing. We were building in boom times, in which the price of our door sash, for example, soared 30 percent between the time we priced it and the day we finally bought it. We were up against a rush of building jobs in which contractors worked like circuit preachers—one day here and the next there. We had to buck the accepted way of doing things. And we roomed, boarded, and paid an apprentice from

Mr. Wright's Taliesin Fellowship in Wisconsin, in addition to paying the architect's fee.

All these things cost us at least two month's delay while we tried to find a contractor, and more delay later.

Because the bids were so extravagantly high, we finally gave up on a general contractor, and let one for the brick and concrete work, another for the plumbing and heating, and hired a carpenter and his crew by the day. And that is risky business unless you know what you are doing. We didn't, but the apprentice, Gordon Chadwick, did. He was an efficient and a watchful taskmaster. He did more actual work than any one man concerned with the building of that house. He was a sensitive and intelligent executor of the master's plan. And as for the value of a dollar, Gordon knew it intimately, and saved us many of them. We feel a warm debt of gratitude to Gordon Chadwick.

We do also to the carpenter, Howard Rickert, one of the few men who understood what it was all about. After one careful study of the blueprints, he became enthusiastic. "This house," he drawled, "is logical."

As the construction proceeded, he enlarged on this verdict. "This," he declared time and again, "is the most logical house I ever built."

There had been predictions, too, from men who claimed, actually, to be heating engineers, that the radiant heating wouldn't work. There were others that the thin walls without studs would not stand long enough to permit completion of the structure, particularly in the part of the living area that was over eleven feet high. There were other baleful warnings that the walls would be cold on the inside; and that the concrete floors would be a dewy lake of condensation in the summer and a rink of frost in the winter.

One of the big thorns in the little minds of these critics (who milled about, taking pictures and notes, and wanting to see the detail drawings) was the ribbon of clerestory windows. The only support for the roof where they ran was a strut the size of your wrist placed every four feet, the width of a window unit. These struts were notched and merely tacked in place.

They rode atop the wall, able to move with it. And to the practitioners of the Cape Cod school of architecture they were pure folly that God would strike down.

In March, 1941, before our house was finished, we had the heaviest snowfall in nearly twenty years. I measured sixteen inches on the flat roof. And of course, as soon as the road back to our woods was open there was another procession of architects to the scene of the anticipated disaster and triumph. What they didn't know was that we had put up a test section of the wall because a building inspector had refused a permit. That wall had carried four times the maximum load that it could ever be called upon to carry.

The other predictions were just as silly. The walls were never cold to the touch inside; there was never a drop of condensation, a crystal of frost, or any other moisture on our floors. In fact, although we were in the woods, we had less trouble with mould on books and shoes than did our friends in the town in conventional houses with cellars.

As for the cost, we built it on the slim income of a newspaperman with one child and not a solitary extra asset. And we did it without incurring a debt that any financing agency would say was beyond our means. But, of course, they didn't help us incur it. Only the fact that the newspaper for which I worked financed homes for its employes enabled us to build when we did.

We got an extraordinary house for an ordinary price and still paid the inevitable price for being pioneers in our area. And what's more, our house came completely furnished: carpets, furniture, stove, and so forth, all for just about the cost of an ordinary one.

When we sold it recently, two small classified ads in Washington papers brought a deluge of shoppers. The house and yard were full for three days. The real estate agent said he had never been so besieged with prospects and telephone calls in his twenty-odd years of selling houses.

Yet the lending agencies were skeptical. Some would not offer any kind of financing for the sale. The others offered considerably less than they would on a Cape Cod number. Yet we sold our house easily at our price, and could have raised it. The price was typical for these times—which means it was high. But we still are occasionally upbraided by friends for not having set it higher.

As for living, it was so far superior an investment that any other kind of house cannot be mentioned with it. It not only thrills one's sense of beauty and of shelter, but it has every virtue of practicality.

The nearly total absence of upkeep is one of the shining attributes of our kind of house. There just ain't no such animal as upkeep. Consider: there is no paint to be cleaned or to be done over every three or four years, at $500 or more per doing. There are no wood floors to be refinished, re-sanded, or re-laid when warped or squeaky. There are no termites, no rats. They can't get into the solid walls, or gnaw through the concrete floor. About the only item you *have* to spend money for, in our house, is wax, and that is cheap and used only on the inside. Outside, the cypress boards are left to weather as they should, and to acquire the soft, silvery gray patina that is one of the enchanting qualities of cypress.

Some of those things also contribute to the ease of doing housework. And we will accept no argument on our flat claim that it is the easiest house in the world to take care of. There are only these surfaces to be cleaned: waxed wood, waxed brick, waxed red concrete, plate glass, and textiles, such as cushions and carpet. There is no cleaning of streaked and sooted walls because radiant heat is clean heat. And the dust that does come in is easily vacuumed off the waxed wood. Even the penciling and crayoning of children are transient things.

In this house, even the dog stays off the furniture—he prefers to sleep on the warm floor. Now it's important that you understand about the warm floor. After living with radiant heat for six years our family will be satisfied with no other. There are warm floors on cold winter mornings. The air temperature is much lower than with other systems, which means it is never stuffy or uncomfortable. The principle of radiant heat is that a warm surface does not absorb your body heat, hence you can have a lower air temperature. For example, we kept our thermostat at 63 degrees. Seventy is far too warm. And, with this system, the temperature is constant.

The question that all this brings up is: "Why did we leave such a house?" The answer is: we moved to a farm, where we can have a larger Frank Lloyd Wright house for a larger family on a larger expanse of this beautiful green earth. And the farm, besides providing the better way of living, will help finance the house the lending agencies won't like.

The Challenge of Being a Taliesin Fellow (1940/1969)

Gordon Chadwick

In 1932 Wright published his autobiography and founded the Taliesin Fellowship. These two landmarks in his career resulted from the re-establishment of his domestic tranquillity, achieved through his marriage to Olgivanna, a strong willed person who aided and encouraged him in these endeavors. The Fellowship eventually consisted of some sixty apprentices. In theory (if not always in practice) their time was divided equally between the drafting room, domestic chores (there was no hired help, except a cook), and learning about construction and the nature of materials (whether by quarrying stone, building buildings, or supervising construction).

In the preceding article we learned that Gordon Chadwick was one of these apprentices. Here he is interviewed by John Pearse.

Were you involved in the design of the Loren Pope House?

No. I wasn't at all involved in the design. The original project had been designed before I ever saw it.

Bullock, Helen D., and Morton, Terry B., eds. *The Pope-Leighey House*. Washington, D.C.: National Trust for Historic Preservation, 1969, pp. 63–76.

What was the design process at Taliesin, once the client pro-vided a general list of wants? What attention would Mr. Wright have given it?

This house was one of a series called Usonian houses that Mr. Wright designed to be built at modest cost. Each house was planned to fit a particular site and to conform to the client's needs. What they had in common was a structural system—Mr. Wright called it the "grammar"—which gave them a family resemblance despite their variety. Certain features, such as the slab floor with radiant heating, the three-layered sandwich wood walls combined with masonry masses, and the flat roofs with overhangs were repeated in all of them.

The plans for each house were accompanied by a Standard Detail Sheet which was applied to all houses of this type and was used over and over again. It was developed, I believe, after the initial Usonian house, the first Herbert Jacobs' house (Madison, Wisconsin), had been built in 1937. Mr. Wright's participation—even on small projects—was more than would be customary in many architectural offices.

I remember watching him as he made revisions to the original plan for the Loren Pope house and worked out the pattern for the perforated boards, which varied from house to house. He was very fond of the recessed batten designs used in the Usonian houses.

How much detail was given on the plans?

Wright plans required interpretation. The Usonian plans were laid out in a two- by four-foot module but without detailed di-mensions. Every time you got to a doorway, a corner or inter-section where special conditions prevailed, the dimensions had to be modified one way or another. Builders always wanted to know why they couldn't have been just like any other plans, i.e., worked out dimensionally. I think Mr. Wright wanted to emphasize the system concept: and the plans cer-tainly looked prettier without dimensions!

Detailed dimensions were given on the Standard Detail Sheet. You had to keep checking back and forth between it and the plans, which was trying for the builder. Of course, there were some things not included on the Standard Detail Sheet which I improvised on the job.

I am interested in the fact that the corners have no emphasis. Why is that?

There is no vertical trim at the corners because Mr. Wright thought of these walls as screens. Vertical trim at the corners would have suggested intermittent vertical support which they do not have. Mr. Wright often spoke of "plasticity" and I suspect this principle is involved here.

How were the three-layered walls constructed?

The sandwich wall was made up of a core (vertical boards or plywood) with roofing felt on both sides. Then horizontal cypress boards and battens were screwed to both sides of the core [diagram 1].

Does a bookcase of that length (99 inches) have a tendency to sag?

That was a tricky problem. There are invisible steel angle brackets under the shelves at intervals; the vertical leg of the angle is concealed behind the interior wall boards. The shelves actually add to the structural stiffness of the walls.

In the living room of the Baltimore house, there was a very long wall without any visible stiffening. After we had made a test for the building department of a four-foot wall section, they asked, "Well, that was a small section of wall; what happens in a long horizontal wall section when there are no corners or stiffeners?" I answered, "We are going to have bookcases built into that long wall which will act as stiffeners." The building inspectors said, "Listen, we've heard of wallpaper holding up walls, but we've never heard of bookshelves holding up walls."

How was the wood finished?

I think that despite Mr. Wright's idea that wood was its own best preservative, we did put Minwax on the exterior, where it was probably wasted and also on the interior walls, which he specified. Paste wax was used on the furniture.

What was used on the concrete floors?

Wax. I think we found a red-colored wax which heightened the red color of the concrete.

Writings on Wright

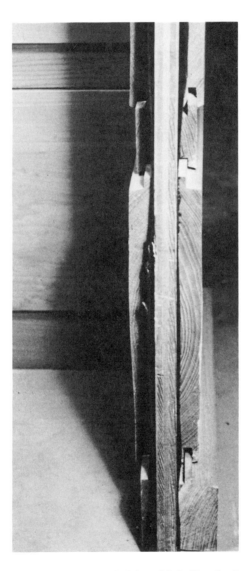

Diagram 1 "The sandwich wall [of a Usonian house] was made up of a core (vertical boards or plywood) with roofing felt on both sides. Then horizontal cypress broads and battens were screwed to both sides of the core." (Courtesy National Trust for Historic Preservation)

Would it be anti-Wright to have a high sheen on the floor?

Not at all. Constant waxing went on at Taliesin where the floors were mostly wood, but even flagstone floors were waxed.

What lighting details were specified by Wright?

In the Loren Pope house, most of the lighting was built in. We installed incandescent bulbs recessed in the overhead trough along the side of the living room. At the indoor trellis over the steps leading down to the living room, we used just ordinary sockets and bare bulbs.

Would you discuss Wright's historical innovations which are reflected in the design of the Loren Pope house?

Radiant heating was a virtually unknown thing at that time. Everybody thought we were crazy to lay wrought iron pipes under the floor. They kept asking, "What if there is a leak? You would have to dig up the whole slab." However, all the pipes were tested for almost a week at approximately 120 pounds of pressure. The normal operating pressure of the system is only 11 pounds, so we had tested far above the maximum that would ever be required. Then we had crushed stone laid around the coils to prevent damage when the concrete was being poured. From a design standpoint, radiant heating was marvelous because getting rid of radiators—then almost universal—reduced visual disturbance.

Built-in lighting, cabinets and bookcases have the same effect. The concrete slab continuing throughout the whole house also contributes to the sense of unity, as does the use of the same wall materials inside and out. In a small house you sense more space when not distracted by extraneous objects, especially here where the interior is kept consistently to horizontal lines and soft natural colors.

A Testament to Beauty (1946/1969)

Marjorie F. Leighey

*What are the reactions of a person who moves into a new
home, and then discovers that it was designed by Wright? The
response of Marjorie Leighey was typical: at first she resisted
when the house seemed to tell her how it might best be used.
Later, tiring of the struggle, she accepted the suggestions it
had to offer, and learned how to obtain more pleasure and enjoyment out of life.*

*The Pope-Leighey house is now a property of the National
Trust for Historic Preservation and has been moved to Wood-
lawn Plantation, Mount Vernon, Virginia, where it may be visited by the public. For information contact the Trust at 1785
Massachusetts Avenue N.W., Washington, D.C. 20036.*

What was it like to *live* there—not just to look at it but to live in
it? *How* did you live? What did it *feel* like?

These are the questions most often asked.

In a sense, living there was a response to the feeling of the
house. That it could have feelings, as well as a feeling, arises
from its real union of the outdoors with the inside, from the
glorious, ever-changing play of patterned sunlight upon the

Bullock, Helen D., and Morton, Terry B., eds. *The Pope-Leighey House.* Washington, D.C.: National Trust for Historic Preservation, 1969, pp. 59–62.

walls and from three paradoxes intrinsic to its structure. Small, yet large because there is no point in the house where one feels spatially bound. Complex with a careful development of patterned and plain areas held together by imaginative and attentive design, yet simple in its forthright presentation of minimal living space. Proud almost to the point of arrogance in boldly declaring itself for what it is and standing thereon, yet humble in never pretending to be other than it is. Such are its paradoxes and they imply mobility or interchangeability. All these qualities—not only the "bringing of the outdoors in" but an actual oneness of the two, not just light in a room but the vivid joy of warm light that moves even as the sun moves and the three seeming contradictions or paradoxes—impart such life to the house that it is not irrational to acknowledge that it has feelings.

At first there is quiet pleasure and thankfulness for being surrounded by something so admirable to look upon.

Then comes the business of living. The need for more storage space is felt almost to desperation. Mr. Wright's own teaching that possessions merely clutter one's life is recalled, and an attempt is made to reduce possessions.

Comes a time of rebellion, an anger at any dwelling-place that presumes to dictate how its occupants live.

Comes the time for decision. Do we truly like the house? Would we rather live here than anywhere else. Again the beauty spoke. It held, compelled. Intelligence was put to work to see how to live within the now-accepted limitations.

A storage shed was built for garden tools and other things still thought of as necessities. More dinner guests were invited as it came to be seen meals could be served differently. Salad, for instance, could be brought to the table as a separate course and served from one large bowl at the table; individual plates did not have to be prepared in the kitchen. Grace and humor could be cultivated when it was necessary for one to back up, to let the other by in a certain narrow passage in the bedroom; it was not necessary to vent the more natural feeling of impatience.

Less obvious and almost inexplicable changes accompanied the change to a simpler way of living. Very subtle were these other changes and the way they came about. To define a thing is to idealize it and at the same time to limit it. Yet it would be an incomplete story to fail to tell how, slowly and progressively, the vital essence of the house began to make its mark on us.

Increasing humility was one of the earliest and most forceful changes. What a blow to self-love to be so often introduced as "my friend I told you about who lives in the Frank Lloyd Wright house," or to have friends bring others to see, not you, but your house!

Possessions continued to be reduced. Instead of many changes of table appointments, only a bare sufficiency was kept. It was humbling to refrain from saying there used to be more or there could now be more, but there is no room for it here. It was equally an offering of humility to refrain from saying that there is good in avoiding luxury, that this is what we chose.

A unique lesson in humility came from the intimate association with the woodland creatures. Flying, crawling, walking, hopping, running, wriggling (snakes, too!)—all kinds of life abounded in the woods. Living with them and watching them day by day and year after year caused a stronger consciousness of one's own creatureliness. Being with them and *being*, too, evoked a gratitude that was a constant song in the heart.

The stripping of accountrements resulted in a stripping of self or self-hood. As one had fewer things, one perforce turned more concentratedly to people. One thought less of whether the custard was perfect—true though it be that cooking is a labor of love—and more of what each guest hoped for from your hospitality. One learned to listen more keenly, to try to hear what the other person really meant and to be ready to share one's own thoughts and hopes as well as to receive others.

Great freedom and ever greater simplicity follow once simplicity has been entered upon as a deliberate choice. Simplicity of possessions gradually expands to include simplicity in manner, action, dress, decoration and interpersonal relationships.

Liberation from things releases deeper imaginative, intellectual and creative processes and there comes to be a unity among the many compartments of life.

In simplicity the individual comes at last to the place from which he started, the human level. He recognizes that it is only as himself, another created being, that he meets all creatures, animal or human. He has an increasing awareness of every aspect of life and that God is the Lord of life. In simplicity he has seen that God is in all and all is of God.

As Mr. Wright called a book *A Testament*, so these words are meant to be a testimony to beauty. Beauty and truth co-mingle in this house. Is it that beauty teaches truth? Does already known truth cause appreciation of the beauty? Who is to know which first illumines or merely supports the other? Here they are, strong and equal and lasting. To have lived for nearly eighteen years where beauty and truth stand like rocks is benison indeed.

The House on the Waterfall (1936/1962)

Edgar Kaufmann, Jr.

Fallingwater, that weekend house built over a waterfall, has captured the imagination of people everywhere. Constructed in 1936, it marked Wright's dramatic comeback from years of semi-retirement. The commission was obtained when the client's son, a former Taliesin apprentice, persuaded his father to hire Wright. Edgar Kaufmann, Jr. here describes the design and construction of this world famous house (figures 17–18).

Fallingwater is open to the public daily, except Monday, from early spring until late autumn but the number of visitors makes reservations advisable. These may be obtained from the Western Pennsylvania Conservancy by writing or telephoning Fallingwater, Mill Run, Pennsylvania 15464.

There was no doubt that Wright was the architect desired, and at our request he came to view the property. The mountains put on their best repertoire to him—sun, rain and hail alternated; the masses of native rhododendron were in bloom; the run was full and the falls, thundering. Wright spent the day, and asked for a survey of the terrain around the falls, clearly the center of our accustomed activities; large boulders and large trees were to be marked on it.

La Casa sulla Cascata di F. Lloyd Wright: F. Lloyd Wright's Fallingwater. Milan: ETAS/Kompass, 1962, pp. 20–25.
Reprinted by permission, Edgar Kaufmann, Jr.

In due time, we received the first sketches for our house—sketches that required hardly any alteration in execution. Amazingly to us, the house did not look toward the falls, it sat above them. It seemed impossible to imagine the result.

But fortunately there was confidence in the architect, and my father, who loved to build, was convinced that he knew how to keep the cost down without using inferior materials. Wright was asked to proceed with the working drawings.

Drawings came, bids were sought, and the advice of structural engineers. The engineers were utterly confused by Wright's architecture which used parapets at the edges of concrete slabs as carrying beams, not as dead weights. His spans were unprecedented, his draughting techniques unfamiliar and thus cryptic. My father was assured that the house could not stand up.

The reports were sent to Wright, and after his explosive response, it was decided to embalm them as a mummy and bury them ceremoniously under the cornerstone of the house; in reality they are immured in a living room wall.

Meanwhile the family scanned every inch of the drawings.

At the eastern, entrance end of the house, at the main bedroom floor, Wright had designed a fancy support for a roof over a terrace. It was the one and only esthetic feature we criticized, and Wright obligingly changed it without demur, but it was to be a source of trouble in the long run. Perhaps because all our requests to Wright (this one excepted) were of a practical rather than an artistic nature, we never found in him the domineering and unbending attitudes that have been widely attributed to him. All our requests were met willingly and simply. At one point, the architect asked if we preferred to build expansion joints in certain concrete parapet walls or to risk cracks which might or might not appear. We risked it; the cracks appeared, nothing serious resulted.

The most westerly extension of the house is an open terrace cantilevered far into space. It is supported by a large reinforced concrete beam on its long axis, and by several transverse ones. The main beam is anchored in the great chimney mass; the lesser ones in a natural boulder nearby. Under the main beam, well back out of sight, a stone supporting wall ran for a number of feet. Here the Pittsburgh engineers were certain of their ground; this was a structure they knew how to calculate, for it was practically independent of the complicated stresses of the main house. They knew that, as it was, the terrace must fall; they knew that just four more feet of that inconspicuous base wall would avoid the disaster. My father called Wright's young apprentice, and ordered the four feet built. Wright himself came around in due course of inspection and said nothing. Another month passed and Wright came again, went over the work with father, and no word of the wall.

At the day's end, over a comfortable drink in the half-finished shell of the house, Father confessed to Wright and said "If you've not noticed it in these last two tours of inspection, there can't be anything very bad about it, architecturally." "E.J.," said Wright, "come with me." They went out to the spot in question and, behold, the top four inches of the additional wall were gone! "When I was here last month," Wright continued, "I ordered the top layers of stone removed. Now, the terrace has shown no sign of failing. Shall we take down the extra four feet of wall?"

The structure is so unusual that, although it is accurately expressed, more familiar preconceptions lead most people to "read" the house wrongly. They think of tall stone walls from which the reinforced concrete projects. In fact, Wright conceived the house as a series of horizontal concrete trays with upturned, stiffening edges; these trays are merely spaced one above the other by short stone masses. Wherever stone and concrete meet, the latter is continuous. Each concrete tray is structural on its *lower* surface; above this, in many areas, is an air space divided by small concrete walls that support a wood floor, finished in flag stones from the nearby quarry.

This captive space allows the stone floors to be well insulated and comfortable even to bare feet. In many rooms there are changes of ceiling level, which are due to Wright's folding the concrete for stiffening, a device similar to that used at the terrace edges. There is practically no structural steel used anywhere in the house, though the window frames at the south end of the living room are augmented by interior T-irons which help [hold] up the heavy cantilevered terrace above.

At last the concrete work of the main house was finished, and time came to remove the forms. The contractor was frightened beyond measure and refused to strike away [the] last timber rising from the falls to the big cantilever. Wright, disgusted, stood next to a workman who struck the post out—and the house stood firm. Over the next few months there was, naturally, a noticeable settlement of the cantilevers. The engineers' dire predictions had so unnerved my father that for years he regularly had levels sighted on the extreme points, until we all learned that the building was in continual, imperceptible motion, expanding and contracting, and that a survey point that fell a fraction one year might rise as much or more the next. Even occasional frost-cracks in the window glass used to increase our fears of structural flaws. But these bogeys vanished with time, and we grew accustomed to the nature of the structure, shedding our fears. The house is his and it is ours, without conflict. Bear Run will always delight and shelter people, demonstrating those victories of space and form and light that remain incorruptible.

Remarks Made by Visitors at the Construction Site, Gregor Affleck House, Bloomfield Hills (1941)

Gregor Affleck

One visitor to another: "I hear that the man who is building this house is an architect and he is crazy."

Another visitor: "Wouldn't you think that fellow could find some level ground to build a house on?"

Visitor to Mr. Affleck: "*We* are going to design our *own* home. We know what kind of a house we like."

Mr. Affleck: "Why don't you write your own music? You know what kind of music you like."

Another visitor to Mr. Affleck: "Did you ever think what would happen if you tried to sell this house?"

Mr. Affleck: "Sure, I think I could sell it. Did you ever think how foolish it is to build a house you don't like so that you can sell it to somebody who will not like it either?"

And Mr. Affleck concludes: "There are only two things wrong with a Frank Lloyd Wright house. People will hardly let you get it built, and will hardly let you live in it when it is done."

Progressive Architecture 27, October 1946, pp. 69, 70.

How a Wright House Came to Be Built (1936/1962)

Paul R. and Jean S. Hanna

During the 1920s, with few commissions in his office, Wright entered into a new period of experimentation. He investigated a variety of shapes in addition to the usual right angle that builders had employed since the beginning of time. At first he tried the 30-, 45-, and 60-degree angles that one finds on an architect's triangles, but acute angles are tight and cramped and not in keeping with the more relaxed and open qualities he sought to achieve. So he turned to obtuse angles and in particular the 120-degree hexagon (the shape of cells in a bee's honeycomb). The hexagon is made up of six equilateral triangles rotated around a common point; two of their contiguous 60-degree angles form the 120-degree inside corners of the hexagon.

Wright also explored the use of arcs and circles, shapes made with a compass. The result produced yet another grammar of form as exemplified in the Guggenheim Museum. Ideas such as these initiated for Wright, and innumerable followers, an entirely new era in the realm of planning and design.

Reprinted from *House Beautiful* 105, January 1963, pp. 57, 106–110.
All rights reserved. Copyright 1963, The Hearst Corporation.

Structural problems also attracted his attention. In the Uson-ian house we noted how he abandoned the traditional bal-loon-frame construction where 2" × 4" vertical studs were sheathed on both sides in order to create a dead air space in between. Instead, Wright substituted a solid "sandwich" wall consisting of a plywood core faced on both sides with roofing paper and horizontal boards (often cypress or redwood) with the same material used both inside and out. These boards were screwed, not nailed, to the core (diagram, p. 62). Strength in this thin wall was gained at corners, or by the an-gular support of bookshelves. In the Hanna house (figures 21–23) the hexagonal cellular shapes provide the integrated structural system. This is what Wright called "integral design."

The Hanna house (1936) is the earliest executed Wright build-ing in which the right angle is completely renounced. There-fore it holds a special place in history. The owners tell their story.

We learned through the daily newspapers of the excitement of students at Princeton University responding to Frank Lloyd Wright when he delivered the Kahn Lectures on "Modern Ar-chitecture." The newspaper stories stirred us to know more, so we placed an advance order for the volume of lectures. When it was available, one day in 1931, we recall that we started in the evening to read the book aloud and finished in the early morning hours. This was the beginning of an architectural vi-rus from which we have never fully recovered.

Our appreciation of the philosophy expressed by Mr. Wright moved us to write him a fan letter, never expecting to receive an answer. Our surprise and pleasure were considerable when we received an answer and an invitation to stop and visit Taliesin if we ever passed through Spring Green, Wisconsin. That summer we drove from New York to Minneapolis and routed ourselves through Wisconsin, hoping that Mr. Wright would not have forgotten his generous invitation.

The Wrights received us cordially and we spent several hours listening to Mr. Wright, drinking in the spell of that lovely place, and getting to know the way his Taliesin Fellowship worked. On taking our leave, we invited him to visit us in our apartment in a Columbia University faculty house.

Twice within the next two years Mr. Wright visited us, once in connection with his exhibit of Broadacre City in New York and again when he lectured at Columbia University. Both times we told him of our desire to have him design a home for us and discussed the kind of life we hoped to live in such a dwelling.

For the summer of 1934 Stanford University invited me [Paul Hanna] to be a visiting faculty member. This proved mutually satisfying to all concerned and resulted in an offer to become a permanent Stanford faculty member, commencing with the summer session of 1935. The first person to be told by telephone that we had accepted the Stanford invitation was Mr. Wright, with the opening statement: "Mr. Wright, we are moving to Stanford and now, at last, you can build us a house!"

In June, 1935, we turned our backs on the East and started West, heading straight for Spring Green and Taliesin. Immediately upon our arrival, Mrs. Wright and the fellowship students took over our children, and we were free to spend hours talking with Mr. Wright about our ideas for our "dream house."

Although we had no clear idea of the type of house we wanted, we did know pretty well what kind of living we wished to enjoy and some pretty definite notions of some of our practical needs. For example, we feel very strongly about fireplaces, comfortable couches, book shelves, glass openings, and bathrooms. We like plenty of each. We wanted large play space for the children, individual bedrooms for the children, each with direct access to a play terrace. We wanted the kitchen so situated that, in the event of servantless days, I

[Jean Hanna] would not feel isolated from family and friends. We needed ample facilities for entertaining large groups.

Perhaps the most ambitious demand we made on Mr. Wright's genius was that he design us a home suitable for all ages. We asked for a house which in all respects would be comfortably livable for a family of five—father, mother, and three children. But we also asked for a house which could be easily altered to suit us (the parents) when the children flew off to their own nests. In short, we wanted a home in which we as parents could live easily and happily *all* our lives. To our everlasting wonder and delight, Mr. Wright was able to achieve this.

The day the first sketches arrived was a memorable one— memorable on two counts: delight and disappointment. The house sketched was so dramatically elegant we were over-whelmed. It was hours before we came down off cloud nine and took a hard, cold look. Regretfully we returned the plans to Mr. Wright with the explanation that we simply couldn't af-ford such a magnificent dwelling and that much as we ad-mired the beauty of the structure, we must have a modest, one-story house. He was not at all perturbed by our response to his hours of drawing. He graciously accepted our explana-tion and went to work on a new concept.

We waited impatiently for a new sketch. The appearance of the honeycomb house, with its unfamiliar 60- to 120-degree angles, should have dismayed us. Instead, we were fasci-nated. This was a whole new idea to us and we immediately set out to study the plan and accustom ourselves to the idea of a basic hexagonal unit of structure. The more we worked with this beehive unit, the more intrigued we were with its possibilities.

We studied the preliminary plans, made amateurish models, and generally lived with the idea for several months while waiting for the university to release the building site we craved. During this period we made many suggestions for al-terations in the plans, based on the peculiar needs of our par-ticular family.

If our suggestions for modifications did not do violence to the fundamental unity of the whole, Mr. Wright incorporated them. If we had an especially good idea, Mr. Wright did not hesitate to adopt or adapt it. On many occasions he said, "that's a fine idea" and, with a twinkle in his eye, "I'll use it in my next house but of course you won't get any credit for it!" All the credit we needed or wanted was the satisfaction that any idea of ours was acceptable to the master designer. Mr. Wright welcomed the cooperation of his clients.

For example, when I [Jean Hanna] protested that there was nothing *in* the kitchen plan, Mr. Wright's response was: "Well, you must know what you want. I've given you the proper shell, now you get busy and fill it in." The same thing with the bath—we filled in the arrangement of the fixtures. Sometimes our pattern was executed; sometimes Mr. Wright suggested a refinement by rearrangement.

Occasionally we would come up with an idea which we felt was brilliant. Instead of scornfully dismissing our tampering with the master's work, Mr. Wright would seize upon the opportunity to educate us. Typically, he would ask (if in our home), "Have you a pencil?" Then he'd sit down and with a few quick strokes would outline our "great" idea. "There now," he'd say, "what do you think?"

Regretfully we were forced to the conclusion that our idea was something less than agreeable. He said; "It is not enough to have an architectural idea in the mind; the mind and the eye must work together. Put your idea on paper and then study it."

We marveled at his patience in this respect. There were times when we obstinately insisted upon having our way. As long as our idea was not too "way out," Mr. Wright would capitulate with this comment: "If you must have it, you must. But you won't like it!" In most such instances we have to confess that he was prophetic.

Phase I of the Construction
Armed with our final plans, we invaded the offices of contractors. We were met with attitudes which varied from stony, abrupt dismissal (what madness is this?) to half-apologetic, half-wistful "how we wished we dared!" It was unbelievable, but no one wanted to take on our house by contract. So we were left with the only alternative: be our own contractor.

We wanted one of Mr. Wright's men to come out and supervise the construction, but all of his men were engaged on other work, and Mr. Wright decided that we ought to try to get some local builder who knew construction in California. Eventually we found Harold Turner who was willing, on a monthly salary, to supervise the construction and we sent him back to Taliesin for consultation.

Asking a carpenter to work on the hexagonal unit was like asking a man suddenly to use his left hand when he had been using his right all his life. Every Monday morning Turner or I [Paul Hanna] went to the hiring hall and picked out five carpenters. By the end of the week, two had quit in disgust or despair, two had been fired, and one remained. This situation prevailed until at long last we would up with five skilled craftsmen, three of whom had been trained in Europe as cabinetmakers. These men were a joy to work with and became, in effect, members of our family.

Phase II
By 1950 we had pushed our publishing ventures (textbooks) to the point where we had paid off phase I. So we talked to Mr. Wright about a hobby shop, a guest house, and storage room. He went to work on new plans.

Phase III
By 1957 our children had moved into their own homes, and we were eager to remove the temporary bedroom walls and expand the space and accommodations to suit the two of us.

"Now," said Mr. Wright, "we will make the back of the house as open as the front." And so he drew the plans detailing the "remodeling" of the bedroom-study area of the house. The four bedrooms and small study vanished and in their place appeared a large master bedroom suite with new bath and dressing rooms and a new bedroom fireplace; a small TV room next to bedroom; a large library with new fireplace; and a powder room.

Phase IV
The final major construction took place in 1961. We wanted more extensive outdoor living space and running water in the garden. We toyed with plans for a strictly Japanese garden, but eventually chose the plan Mr. Wright and his son-in-law, William Wesley Peters, drew for us. This choice seems now the only right one to have made.

Wright's Clients and His Work

Now the one and a half acres are properly provided with house and garden to increase the good life. We can think of no fundamental principle that we would change. The basic design of the house and garden fit the environment organically, and the needs and desires of the owners are fulfilled.

Letters from the Studio of Frank Lloyd Wright (1903–1906)

Charles E. White, Jr.

Few accounts can match the documentary importance of the following letters. They record Wright's method of design while creating his famed prairie houses early in the century. Written by an apprentice, and illustrated with sketches, they also include remarks on the organization of Wright's office and various members of his staff.

An interesting footnote to history is found therein. It concerns a hitherto unknown offer made by the Architectural Record *(in 1903) to devote an entire issue to Wright's work—with the text to be written by whomever Wright might choose. We are further informed that Wright had considered Russell Sturgis, the renowned architect-critic, for this task. In the end however Wright prepared the article himself, "In the Cause of Architecture," published in 1908. He had little confidence that Sturgis, or any other American critic, sufficiently understood his work. He was quite right—this is evident on reading Sturgis' critique of the Larkin Building (see part III).*

Journal of Architectural Education 25, Fall 1971, pp. 104–112.
Courtesy of The Library, University of Oregon.

Elgin, Illinois, November 16, 1903
Dear Walter Willcox,

Every day since my arrival in the west, I have intended writing but have had so much visiting to do with my family, that the time has slipped away. I have seen Mr. Wright, and had many good talks with him. He is very busy—has seven draftsmen.

Wright has done some fine work the past year. The Architectural Record has offered him a complete number for January, with whoever he may choose to write the article. Do not think he will be ready with his stuff by that time, however. Think he will choose Russell Sturgis, as he says he would like to know what he would say about him. You mustn't be surprised if I write a great deal about Wright from time to time—don't get bored. Think you will be interested, though.

W. tells me to stop reading books for a while, and do nothing but study nature and sketch. He says to continually and eternally sketch the forms of trees—"a man who can sketch from memory the different trees, with their characteristics faithfully portrayed, will be a good architect"!

W. says all of his design was suggested by the prairies on which they are built—he is "thoroughly saturated with the spirit of the prairie"—and doesn't think he could easily design work for a hilly country. Am quite impatient to see what he will do with the Montreal house, as it is to be built on the side of the mountain. I think he is a little puzzled, for he talks of going up into the mountains for a two weeks trip, to "group his ideas." It is a splendid chance. One hundred thousand to spend, and absolutely no requirements.

Cordially,
Charles White Jr.

Oak Park, May 13, 1904
It is actually so long since I have written a letter that the pen seems queer and unnaturally unwieldy in my fingers. . . . Now let me see what news I have for you this time—with so many weeks to review there ought to be something.

We have [presently working in the studio] Drummond, Byrne, Griffin, Miss Mahony, and Miss Roberts.

Miss Roberts works most of the time on ornamental glass; Miss Mahony is modelling for a fountain for the Dana house at Springfield. Griffin is general practical man, writer of specifications and the like, while we remaining three are draftsmen in general.

One late acquaintance which gives me much pleasure, is Richard Bock, sculptor, who has moved to Oak Park, and will occupy the balcony. He has decided to put himself under Mr. W's criticism for a period, as it is his ambition to become a strictly architectural sculptor. He will do the work for the Buffalo building, and then such other work as he can get from other sources. He's just returned from St. Louis, where he has some work for the fair, and says that the Chicago fair was far superior architecturally.

Russell Sturgis came very recently and spent a few hours. He is a sweet old chap of about seventy, every inch a gentleman. He is medium height, thick set, with a well trimmed white beard, very spry and energetic. As it happened, I was engaged at some work that Mr. Wright wanted him to see, so he came over to my corner, and I was the only fortunate draftsman who was introduced to him. Mr. Wright does not think that he understands the work of the Studio, so will try and get some younger man to write the article for the Record. The publication has been once more set for July, but it may have to wait awhile longer.

We have much new work in the office. Several residences around Chicago, Peoria, Madison etc., and the balance of the houses in Buffalo. I am working almost entirely on Buffalo houses. So much for the general news—and now I want to explain if I can some of Mr. W's ideas regarding architecture, sculpture, painting, and music.

When W. first came out of Sullivan's office, he very naturally put into his work much of S's method, and not a little of his ornament. Then came the period of transition, when he was trying to break away from Sullivanism, and casting about for methods of self-expression. His works of those days were interesting—and somewhat above the work of the average man, tho lacking the stability and refinement of his present work. It was over elaborated—covered with "ornamental ornament." His tendency of the last two years has been to simplify and reduce to the "lowest elements" (as he says) his designs. His grammar, which he may be said to have invented, is such as he used in the Winslow house, consisting of a base, a straight piece of wall up to the second story window sills, a frieze from this front to the roof, and a cornice with a wide overhang. He never cuts anything above the cornice line, like dormers.

Here is his grammar, roughly sketched, and all his buildings today are built along these lines

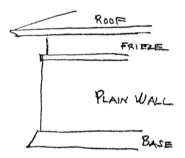

Wright's greatest contribution to Architecture, I think, is his unit system of design. All his plans are composed of units grouped in a symmetrical and systematic way. The unit usually employed is the casement window unit of about these proportions.

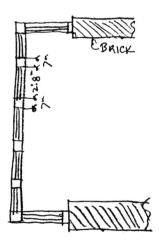

These units are varied in size and number to suit each particular case, and the unit decided upon, is consistently carried through every portion of the plan. His process in getting up a new design is the reverse of that usually employed. Most men outline the strictly utilitarian requirements, choose their style, and then mold the design along those lines, whereas Wright develops his unit first, then fits his design to the requirements as much as possible, or rather, fits the requirements to the design. I do not mean by this that he ignores the requirements, but rather that he approaches his work in a broad minded architectural way, and never allows any of the petty wants of his client to interfere with the architectural expression of his design. The petty wishes are taken care of by a sort of absorption and suppression within the scope of the plan as a whole, and are never allowed to interfere with the system, or skeleton of the house. Here is one of the Buffalo houses, as it was roughly sketched out. On second thought, I will make or get a sketch at the Studio tomorrow, showing it on a larger scale. Will also send some blueprints from some old negatives which may be of interest, with notes explaining them on the back.

The studio is again torn up by the annual repairs and alterations. Twice a year, Mr. W. rearranges and changes the different rooms. He says he has gotten more education in experimenting on his own premises, than in any other way.

He is now putting down a monolith floor, throughout, consisting of wood plup and a cement imported from Greece. Has also torn out some partitions, cut in ceiling lights etc. The place has been torn up so long that I haven't had an opportunity to take any photographs. Will get some when we get settled once more.

May 19, 1904

This is another little opportunity to write, Walter, which I seize with much pleasure. . . . Last evening I got home to find a dinner party on the books, in honor of my twenty-eighth birthday anniversary. . . .

In the first installment of this chat I believe I was speaking of Wright and some of his ideas. Regarding architecture, the sketch plan of the Martin house, will show his unit scheme of construction—huge brick piers, with glass and brick curtain walls between [figures 3–4]. Note the symmetry of the design, and see what beautiful work it is to develop. Never gets dry and uninteresting.

The entire Martin (Buffalo) house is regarded as one of W's best opportunities. A charming lot, with a group of three buildings (Barton house, Martin house, stable and conservatory). The Barton house is just about completed. I am now working on the Martin house. Stable plans have just been sent them.

Barton and Martin are both members of the firm of Larkin Soap Company. We have also nearly completed a house for Heath, of the same concern. You see the Larkin work has opened up a great bunch of stuff. Martin is also interested in Martin & Martin of Chicago for whom we have recently designed the stove polish factory.

Will note a few of Wright's ideas as they occur to me.

All features of the design have some recognition of the plan. He never supports an overhead beam this way—

But always this way—

In other words, he never uses attached columns or pilasters. In this day of steel, he uses the arch very rarely and recognizes the lintel construction, by strong horizontal lines throughout the building. He is so adverse to the arch, that in a barrel vaulted room, he usually tries to eradicate the effect of the sloping lines of the tympanium, by horizontal architectural lines in the decoration, or trim. He enjoys the soffit of the vault, but dislikes the tympanium. A short time ago he told us that he has a scheme for the next vaulted room as follows.

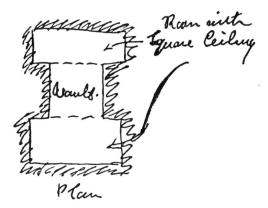

Thus he will leave only the soffit of the vault, as the tympanium will be done away with. He never uses chandeliers—always concealed, ceiling lights, or brackets (partially necessary by low ceilinged rooms). Griffin has just gotten up a scheme for a combination bracket fixture like this

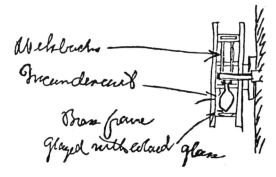

This case or lantern lifts off. When in place conceals the lights within. These fixtures will contain gas and electric, or two electric lights, distributed about the room, the combination cannot be recognized from the electric lights. The lantern can be lifted off to light the gas. This provides for gas lighting, and still all the fixtures are the same in appearance throughout the house. Here is another Wright fixture

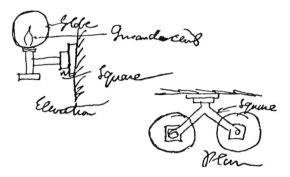

Note how everything is in simple square planes in keeping with the horizontal and perpendicular lines of the house, while the angle in the plan, repeats the shape of the roof. Thus everything throughout the house is in the same feeling. When he designs glass, ironwork, furniture, fixtures, etc., he first analyzes the type of his building, and designs in the same spirit (no searching of books for stereotyped details). The fact that the design is so constantly and systematically correct throughout, removes him from the "merely odd" class, like Maher and a few others. He has a reason for everything he does. . . .

Hastily, regards from us both,
Charles

[Editor's note: When the following extract was written, Charles E. White, Jr., had left Wright's employ in order to practice on his own.]

Oak Park, March 4, 1906

Dear Old Walter:

The chief thing at Wright's is of course Unity Church, the sketches of which are at last accepted, after endless fighting. We have all pleaded and argued with the committee, until we are well nigh worn out. All hands are working on the working drawings. The building will cost about thirty-five thousand. Will send you pictures and description [figures 9–10].

My personal feeling is that for a liberal church we at last have a design that is beautiful and consistent. The Unitarian idea calls for an institution rather than a church, and this leaves

Wright free to follow out his natural inclinations. It seems to me that his design marks an epoch in the architecture of the entire country. It has all the chaste beauty of a Greek temple, and much of the sublimity of your favorite Taj Mahal. How I wish you could see the plaster model which has been made. The scale is tremendous, and the proportions ideal. Of course in plan, some room is wasted for architectural effect, but they have more seats than they really require. Rather than say "room is wasted" I prefer to say that some seats have been donated to the more honorable purpose of Art in its highest sense. This building, I prophesy, will be admired for generations to come, as a beautiful and fitting memorial to the service of God, and the betterment of mankind. It will probably be adversely criticized from one end of the land to the other, but I think it will be one of the things that will live on. It has a virile quality that cannot die. The building will be cast in solid concrete, finished on the outside like a sidewalk. The design is economical in the extreme. I do not know of a church of the same area that can be built in masonry for the same price. Just think, that miserable little Gothic chapel I designed in Boston, cost twenty-five thousand! The motif, as you will note, is an evolution of Wright's studio. An entrance in a link connecting a dominant, and subordinate mass.

There has not been much other work of importance at Wright's. The Montreal house is all off. They have purchased an old house in the town, and W. is getting out plans for altering it. He has had a few houses of five-thousand-dollar size, and as he always loses money on such, it cannot be said that his affairs have been particularly prosperous lately. If it hadn't been for the Buffalo building, he would have been in straits long ago. He made a great mistake in going abroad just when he did.

Walter Griffin has resigned, and will practice in Chicago. His place is taken by Wright's brother-in-law, who comes from a position in Armor's Beef concern. A good businessman (no experience in architecture) and a fine fellow. Suppose he will eventually write specifications and superintending. Willatzen has resigned to take a position with Robert Spencer at thirty dollars. He wants to save up some money, and go abroad for a year. Hardin is a new man, who left the University of Illinois after one year. His tuition was paid by a fellow townsman in

Texas, who has thrown him over since he has become so "degraded" as to go into Wright's. Marion Mahony has been doing great work (the Unity Perspectives are hers). I think she is one of the finest in the country at this class of rendering. . . .

Yours,
Charles

The Taliesin Fellowship (1932/1979)

Edgar Tafel

From the letters of Charles E. White, Jr., we learned something about Wright, his method of design, and of life at the Oak Park studio early in this century. Thirty years later many of these questions again were treated, but this time for the period of the Taliesin Fellowship. The writer, Edgar Tafel, joined that group when it was founded in 1932, and remained for nine years. The Fellowship, in the traditional sense, was neither an architect's office nor a school yet for Wright it established an environment sympathetic to his needs. His creativity through-out those years—from the age of sixty-five to ninety-one— owed much to these congenial surroundings.

The grand plan for the Taliesin Fellowship was outlined by Mr. Wright in his first prospectus, 1932, and was updated from time to time. It was originally planned to include "seven and seventy workers in the arts"—Mr. Wright, six "honor men hav-ing the status of seniors in music, painting, sculpture, drama, motion, and philosophy," and seventy apprentices. There were also to be "technical advisers" for crafts and visiting "leaders in thought" from many countries. Mr. Wright empha-sized the importance of integrating work and constant contact

Tafel, Edgar. *Apprentice to Genius: Years with Frank Lloyd Wright.* New York: McGraw-Hill, 1979, pp. 137, 138, 140, 141, 143, 144, 145, 146, 148, 152, 160, 161, 162, 164, 165, 167, 23, 132, 134, 22, 23.
Used with the permission of McGraw-Hill Book Co., copyright 1979, McGraw-Hill Book Co.

with nature and growth. Apprentices were to live and work in buildings they had constructed or renovated using native Wisconsin materials. From the 1937 brochure:

And with a more complete consciousness of the design of the whole, materials are taken directly from their sources: felling trees, sawing them into lumber, turning lumber into structure, trusses, furniture, block carvings; quarrying rock and burning lime to lay the hewn stones in the wall; sculpting them; plastering; digging; working in the field, planting and harvesting; making roads. Planning, working, and philosophizing in voluntary cooperation in an atmosphere that has the integrity of natural loveliness.

Along with these activities Mr. Wright envisioned furniture design and manufacturing; weaving; photography; printing and publication of monographs, books, music, drawings, and block prints. He planned studios for ceramics, wood, and glass and shops to sell handcrafts. He hoped to sell designs to American industry for mass production. The design force was impelling him, as always, to generate an authentic American culture.

Mr. Wright needed advice and help on the organization of the daily routines for the community he was planning. For this he turned to Mrs. Wright. In her years as a student and instructor at Georgi Gurdjieff's Institute for the Harmonious Development of Man, in France, Mrs. Wright learned the patterns of living in a closed society run on a strict routine by a master with a powerful philosophy. This experience gave her the background to organize the operation of Taliesin and to bring another dimension to life in the Fellowship. In this way, her experience with Gurdjieff did influence the form of the Fellowship and some of the activities envisioned at the beginning. Mrs. Wright was the force that kept the Fellowship in working order, from the very start. A remarkable woman.

Yet Taliesin never became the close-living, totally organized community that Mr. Wright had planned and spelled out in the prospectus. Mr. and Mrs. Wright were feeling their way at the beginning. They couldn't have had a clear idea how the Fellowship would really go.

In the early days we had a large turnover of apprentices. Life at Taliesin was not for everyone. Mr. Wright never went out and recruited apprentices, never did any advertising. Whenever he lectured, however, he talked about the school.

We all started out as paying apprentices, but in 1932, after we'd been at Taliesin for just a few months, a nationwide "bank holiday"—suspending all banking functions—was imposed. Most of the parents were affected by the Depression and couldn't afford the fees even after the banks reopened. Mr. Wright never sent anyone away. He went on lecture tours. He wrote and received royalties on his books. And from time to time, new apprentices brought in new money.

Mr. and Mrs. Wright made attempts at organizing daily life at Taliesin, but only the meal schedules worked. The routine of no routine—that was life at the Fellowship. We dealt with each day's important matters as they came up, though the long-range building projects were handled more systematically. There were always more things to do than hands and money to get them done. Winter always came too soon. Summer always came too soon. Time and seasons were always against us, and we were always behind. Mr. Wright felt that time was pushing him, that it was behind him trying to overtake him, and that we'd never be finished. As a result, he projected that kind of frenzy onto us. Always.

The big bell rang first at 6:30 A.M. to wake us, the second bell at 7:00 called us to breakfast. We had to be in the dining room before 7:30, when the kitchen closed. In the beginning, servants worked in the kitchen, took care of the linens, and served us at the tables. However, the Wrights soon found that they couldn't afford this service. So we all took turns in the kitchen, waiting on tables, and cleaning up. Those of us who'd attended summer camp took to it well enough; the rest had to learn.

After breakfast, duties were assigned, some continuing from days before, some new. We might do a dozen different jobs in the morning—garden for a while, drive the tractor for road grading, dig a ditch or trench for footings to go under a new wall, drive down to the river for a load of sand, help rescue a car that was stuck. One of the toughest and coldest jobs in winter was to cut ice in the river and haul the blocks to the icehouse, where we packed them in layers, sawdust between the blocks. There was plenty of sawdust from our own sawmill.

In spring we plowed and planted, fixed the buildings, trying to stop the leaks, cleared up the dead leaves with rakes.

In summer we cultivated the crops in the big garden on the side of the hill. The crops were nearly enough to feed us all, with enough left over to sell some of the vegetables.

By August we settled into our weekend activities with some regularity. Saturday was cleaning-up day at Taliesin, washing windows and sweeping. We gathered varieties of flowers and arranged them everywhere. Even in the drafting room. In the evening we went over to Hillside, where dinner was served in the theatre. One or two people stayed at Taliesin in case of fire or other emergency. After dinner there was entertainment— the chorus sang, there were a few piano selections, and we'd have a film.

Mr. Wright loved picnics as a change of pace. On Sunday morning—by about 11:00 or 11:30, we'd assemble in the tea garden for a picnic trek. The cooks had already prepared everything. We'd pile into five or six cars and drive out through the valley until Mr. Wright found a spot he liked. Always a new place. He'd go up to a farmer and ask permission for us to have a picnic on the hillside. Everybody went to the picnics. (No one could get out of it.) After we settled, Mr. Wright would say a few words of wisdom and then we had lunch. After eating, we'd split up into groups of friends. About 1:30 or so, we drove back to Taliesin. The afternoon was given over to visitors; each week a few apprentices would serve as guides. The rest of us had the afternoon free, until about 6:00 P.M., when we were all invited to the Wrights' for an aperitif, a glass of wine, followed by dinner in their living room. After dinner, the musical apprentices performed, usually playing Mr. Wright's favorites. I'd be asked to play "Jesu, Joy of Man's Desiring" and a Brahms Intermezzo. Sometimes I'd squeeze in a Debussy prelude, which he didn't really like.

Our first experience with wine at Taliesin was a disaster. We made a huge batch of wine in the first year of the Fellowship, had a bit too much, and ended up on the roof. Next morning, Mr. Wright called us together and asked who'd had more than one glass. We all stepped forward. He asked who'd had more than two glasses and quite a few apprentices took another step forward. Then he said, "More than three?" Four of us advanced still further. He fired us on the spot, saying he had to set an example for the others. He took us back to his office, gave a lecture on organic architecture, told us to mind our ways and stay.

Autumn tasks meant preparing for winter. The apples had to be brought in, and we made our own cider. We filled the root cellar with vegetables. We began to keep fires going in the fireplaces, until it got cold enough to turn on the boilers. There was a marvelous earthy aroma—inside and out—of burning oak logs all through the winter. In addition to the farmers who worked at Taliesin, there were always one or two apprentices who had a farm background. They were the ones who got up at 5:00 A.M. to milk the cows. We also had goats and goats' milk for cheese. A big white cotton bag used to hang in the kitchen, separating the curds into cheese. This was the real organic life. We were close to nature all the time.

Those first winters, we took turns going to the woods to cut trees for building lumber. Mr. Wright bought his wood from neighboring farmers, "on the stump." We helped fell the trees and we trimmed the branches. Logs would be snaked to the road, rolled up on to a flatbed truck, trundled to Hillside, and dropped on the uphill side of the sawmill. We helped the professional sawyers hump the logs along with big tongs and lug away the lumber as it came from the saw—beams, framing studs, planks, boards. Bark slabs were cut in two-foot lengths to stoke the boilers and fireplaces. We sawed our own lath.

The wood came dripping wet from the mill, oozing sap; it had to dry out before use. But lath had to be wetted before it could be plastered, so why not use the wood green? Nature had soaked it for us. Do it all in one operation, said Mr. Wright. It didn't work. The lath twisted as it dried. Many walls had to be redone.

We also worked the quarries—limestone for Taliesin, sandstone for Hillside, cutting out the blocks or sawing or splitting them loose, cleaving them into building size. Flat hewn stones, varying in size and thickness—ashlar. To bed the stones there had to be lime mortar, and since cement was too expensive we built a lime kiln. Obtaining sand was much simpler. We just dug it out of the river bed.

In those first days there were two of us to a room, but later most of us had our own rooms and a little time to personalize our domains. Every so often, Mr. and Mrs. Wright would make a tour to see how we had designed our living spaces. If my room happened to be a mess that day, as it usually was, Mr. Wright would call me in. Someone would say, "Edgar, Mr. Wright wants to see you in his office." I'd go at once, fearful and anxious. Sometimes the reprimand was short. If he was good and angry, the lecture took longer. In any case, it always seemed to end with a few remarks about organic architecture. We quickly learned to turn away his anger by slipping in a question about Oak Park days. This lengthened the lecture but made it more enjoyable.

After dinner, unless we were busy working on a project in the drafting room, our time was our own. Lights went off about ten at night—when the power was cut at the hydroelectric plant. After that it was candles and kerosene lamps. In the early days before we had public electric power, electricity was generated from the hydro machine at the dam below Taliesin.

Descriptions of apprentices out in the fields, making concrete or milking cows or driving the tractor, probably make it seem that little was being done in the drafting room—that architecture, the real purpose of the Fellowship, was giving way to farming. During the first three years or so of the Fellowship, there actually wasn't much to do in the drafting room. The only real project was the Willey house. Jobs did not start coming in until about 1936. Mr. Wright felt in those years that he was getting ready. He had infinite faith that the Fellowship would grow into a working organization, that the nation's economy would revive, and that he would have created architects to build for the revitalized nation.

In the drafting room, as elsewhere at Taliesin, we learned by doing. In the beginning, with senior draftsmen to supervise, Mr. Wright had us copying drawings of his early buildings and working on drawings for the rooms under construction at Hillside. In a sense, it was a make-work program. When I arrived [in 1932], the drawings for the Hillside drafting room had just been completed. I was assigned to copying rooms of the Imperial, to making plates showing the hotel's layout and furnishings.

We never knew when Mr. Wright might come into the drafting room. Any time, any day. The drafting room was his center of everything. We'd be working, seated on benches covered with animal hides, and suddenly the door would creak. We could tell it was Mr. Wright—he always cleared his throat before entering. We stood up out of deference; those who were standing turned to face him. It was always an emotional and sometimes even an electrifying experience to have him there. Those sharp eyes!

To reach his office, he had to walk through the drafting room—but he would never walk straight through. He'd stop at drafting tables to review the work, to make additions and changes. To go back to his quarters, he had to walk through the drafting room again. When the bell rang for lunch, he often kept right on working.

Mr. Wright had a formidable power of concentration. Yet he'd occasionally grow restless. After drawing for a while, he might go over to the bench next to the fireplace and lie down, his cane beside him, maybe a book under his head. An apprentice in the drafting room would put a finger to his lips and warn the others not to make a sound: Mr. Wright was napping. He'd wake with a start—he never got up sluggish—and storm back to his work. Sometimes he'd change everything on the drawing. His preliminary drawings for a project were filled with lines. Sometimes he'd throw away the drawing—push it aside and let it drop on the floor.

Mr. Wright was marvelous to work with. His sense of mission permeated his thinking and the drawings that he spread out before us—ever repeating that a better world will grow out of better creative solutions, better design. Each time he sat down at the drafting board, we sensed the power of his intent. "Every change is for the betterment," he'd tell us reassuringly. He always felt he was right. Yet he always changed everything. Each day we feared that he'd change what he had settled the day before. We'd point out as he started revising a drawing, "But Mr. Wright, yesterday you decided it *this* way!" His answer was standard. "That was all right yesterday, but it's not all right today." He never left anything alone. He no sooner got something going than he'd upset it all. We'd be working on a project in the drafting room when he suddenly decided to decorate a room with branches. He would send the nearest apprentice off to the woods to collect foliage.

He had a remarkable memory for the instructions he'd given us on drawings. If we drew a detail that differed the least bit from what he'd asked for, he caught it immediately. He couldn't tolerate the slightest mismeasurement or faulty coordination.

Sometimes we left architectural magazines open for him on the drafting tables. He never suspected we were tricking him into a reaction. At least, he never let on. We learned how to evoke Mr. Wright's better nature. If a detail in a drawing didn't work, the best way to get his help was to say, "Mr. Wright, I'm in trouble. I can't get this detail to work out right." He'd sit down and muse over it, humming and singing to himself. "Let's see. . . . Well, not so much of a problem. We'll fix it."

Mr. Wright's accent was pure Midwest. The voice had great strength, coming from deep in the chest. He rarely talked in a whisper. How could he? He was always claiming, declaiming, pontificating. He loved to bellow out a tired phrase; "America is the only country to have gone from a state of barbarism to a state of decadence with no intervening culture." The simplest statement, from his tongue, became a graven, immutable truth for all ages, even if it was just about the weather.

He delighted in polemic and invective. He stirred the public and goaded the press by sounding off on any social, political, or cultural issue of the moment—even architecture. Part of the turbulence was just for fun and for the sake of drama. Being dramatic was a sure way to make the American people listen.

He knew the value of architectural publicity—not only to bring in clients, but to make Americans examine their way of living. He wanted to bring them his vision of "true" democrecy. This was the kernel of Mr. Wright's "mission." Architecture, whatever else it represented to him, was the means to realize that vision.

He rarely turned down a speaking engagement. He'd go off on talks to women's organizations and service clubs. He sometimes accepted college lectures at establishment institutions, where he found sponsorship for his renegade philosophies only in the student organizations. He'd get all the students on his side first, then he'd shake up the faculty, who would protest about him for the rest of the semester.

Mr. Wright was marvelous with an audience. He got a kick out of the response evoked by his more outrageous commentary. On stepping up to the podium, he would look at his audience and say, "I've seen most American cities, most of them ugly, and now that I've seen yours, I'm convinced it's by far the ugliest." Rotarians were ruffled by him; he had their attention from the very start.

In public, he generally wore a trim porkpie hat, which he sometimes abandoned for a soft beret. A tailor in Chicago made up the clothing Mr. Wright designed for himself. He never dressed outlandishly, but he certainly had a definite style. There were his capes, which made him appear seven feet tall when he swirled them over his shoulder, and he always wore stiff, high-starch detachable shirt collars.

Mr. Wright never just walked. He strutted. He marched. He strode. He entered a room like a king entering his audience chamber, Mrs. Wright behind him like a queen. Usually, too, he carried a cane, but that was a mere stage prop, a mace, used for effect. All his movements showed a natural, animal grace.

Everything about Mr. Wright's stature and presence showed that he clearly thought of himself as a living legend and loved acting out the role. And each new day was for new enjoyment.

Part III

American Assessment (1897–1912)

The number of writings on Wright published in America during his first forty or more years of practice is amazingly slight, with the most significant of these dating from the period 1897 to 1912. The earliest article, in 1897, appeared after House Beautiful *"visited" his Oak Park home; two years later they wrote about his studio. These chatty, descriptive pieces are rich in documentation for the historian who seeks information on the original design, color, and furnishing of these important structures. Then, in 1900, the* Architectural Review *of Boston published a major review of Wright's budding career written by his close friend Robert Spencer. No article of major importance appeared again until March 1908 when* Architectural Record *published Wright's manifesto "In the Cause of Architecture" and, in April, Sturgis' caustic critique of the Larkin Building. Both articles were profusely illustrated. The same year* Architectural Review *printed Thomas Tallmadge's historical study of "The 'Chicago School,'" which included the work of Wright and his midwest contemporaries (including Tallmadge), a group that we have come to call the Prairie School. Wright at this time was building such masterpieces as the*

Robie, Roberts, and Coonley houses, and Unity Temple was nearly complete.

But these events of 1908 heralded little for the future. In spite of the fact that Architectural Record *published a comparative study of two houses by Louis Sullivan and Wright in 1911, and a book review by Montgomery Schuyler of the Wasmuth folios in 1912, American recognition of Wright had all but ceased— however ill-informed much of it had been. Yet one thing is worse than bad reviews, and that is no reviews at all. This, except for coverage on Taliesin and the Imperial Hotel, was typical of the situation after 1912. By then, however, Europe had discovered Wright.*

No part of this book proved so vexing to edit as this. With the exception of Spencer's perceptive piece (probably prepared with the aid of Wright) little was published that merits thoughtful reading. Yet this is part of the historical scene, and as such deserves our brief consideration. It portrays the discouraging, often embittering, situation faced by Wright, and demonstrates precisely how the professional journals and critics failed to properly comprehend his work.

The Work of Frank Lloyd Wright (1900)

Robert C. Spencer, Jr.

Written at the close of the nineteenth century, this perceptive analysis not only summarizes but seems to predict the course of Wright's career. It is hard to believe that the fully mature, post-1900, prairie house did not exist. Equally unexpected is Spencer's sensitive treatment of Wright's Froebel kindergarten training and its impact on his work.

Spencer and Wright, with other Prairie School architects, shared office space at Steinway Hall. Thus Wright probably furnished some of these ideas.

When published by Architectural Review *in 1900 (and reprinted as a booklet in 1964) nearly eighty small illustrations enriched an equally generous text, here much reduced in length.*

Few architects have given us more poetic translations of material into structure than Frank Lloyd Wright. To this young man, whose career has but begun, has been accorded the space in this issue of the *Review*, that the original and varied work which he has done might count as a unit for the cause of independent architectural thought and original native effort. That some of this work has been the designing of simple houses of the less costly sort, does not detract from, but rather adds to the interest which it should inspire.

These modest buildings are more interesting than nine-tenths of the so-called "important work" of the present time. They embody new thought and new ideas. They have life. They express clearly and consistently certain ideals of home and of quiet, simple home life, and are solutions of problems which have been developing slowly among our people of the intelligent middle class.

A careful study of his work will show that while Mr. Wright has an evident love for the horizontal dimension and the horizontal line, he seldom employs it except in sympathy with masses in which the horizontal dimension exceeds the vertical, and that whether the scheme of wall treatment be horizontal or vertical there is almost invariably a base or stylobate of sufficient size to unify his masses and support the spring of the building from the ground with which it seems firmly and broadly associated. The simple matter of the size and scale of this stylobate, even on the small house, as compared to the weak and puny base of the average building, is a very pleasing departure from precedent and gives to these buildings a touch of the quiet dignity of the old Greek temples.

In the treatment of his walls the ruling idea is that of a plain or subordinately treated surface between two terminals, the base or pedestal and the cornice or frieze; a beginning, an upward growth and an ending. It is one of the faults of the average "drawing-board architect" that he neglects or forgets the third dimension in his buildings. In the work we are considering the value of this element is everywhere recognized and a satisfying feeling of solidity and depth not only prevails, but the treatment of reveals and other surfaces opposed to the main wall surfaces is carefully studied, and where ornament is employed the decoration of the one is intimately and organically related to or a direct continuation of the decoration of the other.

About two miles west of Oak Park in the suburb of River Forest, there are several examples of Mr. Wright's work, one of which, the Winslow house, is more than worth a pilgrimage to see. In fact, it is the broadest, the most characteristic and the most completely satisfying thing that he has done. This oppor-

American Assessment (1897–1912)

tunity came to him in the third [*sic*: first] year of his independent practice and is the only site beautiful in itself that has yet
come into his hands. Upon the chosen site Nature has been at
work for years building the wonderful elm which, with its
spreading arms and feathery sprays, was destined to shade
this house, and the character of the house was somewhat determined by the circumstance of this tree [figure 1]. The sympathy that has been firmly established between them is felt by
the cultivated and uncultivated. The street facade, as will be
seen in the photograph, is simple with a breadth of treatment
that carries the exquisite refinement of its detail with perfect
dignity. Within the grounds to the rear we are afforded a more
intimate knowledge of the conditions of life within and the
scheme becomes less reticent and is more picturesque without sacrificing the quiet formality of the whole. The impression conveyed by the exterior is the impression conveyed
by the elm. A certain simple power of an organic nature that
seems to have as much right to its place and is as much a part
of the site as the tree. The analogy begins there and continues,
for the details of the house are as much in their place and as
consistent in themselves and in relation to each other, as the
whole house is to its surroundings. A layman has said that his
first view of this house gave him the same thrill that he felt
when listening for the first time to an orchestra. The stable in
the rear, with its background of tall trees, one of which shoots
upward through the eaves, is a classic little gem in keeping
with the house, and contains the printing shop of the Au-
vergne Press, where Mr. Winslow and Mr. Wright printed their
beautiful edition of Wm. C. Gannett's "House Beautiful."

If I were making a plea for the kindergarten idea in education, I
could adduce no better living example of its value as a factor
in the development of the artistic faculties than by referring to
the subject of these pages. He is one of very few in our profession who have enjoyed that training. As a child in Boston he
was given by his mother the benefit of the Froebel system of
training the eyes to see, the brain to think and the hands to do.
To this fortunate early training as a beginning she ascribes his
instinctive grasp of niceties of line, form and color. And no
more fortunate circumstance could have befallen him than his
schooling with Mr. Sullivan, himself an independent and close
student of nature. It is certainly true that the highly conventionalized, the quiet, consistent structural element, is always

present in his composition, modifying and quieting the most naturalistic motives. Nature, who knows the most rigid and subtle geometry, as well as the most voluptuous freedom of, and apparent confusion of form, is the source to which he has always gone for inspiration. If not to nature at first hand, then to those marvellous interpreters of nature, the Orientals and the Japanese. There is nothing capricious or incomprehensible in the methods and ideals involved in the development of this distinctive treatment of ornament. It is a natural outgrowth of structure, an organic part of a whole, which without it would be incomplete and lacking in expression. Each building has its own expression and its own specific type of generic decoration. There is no mere applied ornament. The makers of detail in *papier maché* and *carton pierre* would all starve if this conception of the nature of ornament became general. The building is conceived as a perfect and complete organism. According to this conception there must be intimate and organic relation between ornament and structure, between surface decoration and decorated surface, between one phase of ornament and another. A richly developed surface should not appear as background and ornament. The ornament should be *of* the surface, not *on* the surface and there should be no tangible background at all. That is the spirit in which the rich frieze decorations of the Winslow, Heller and Husser houses are designed. Analyze, for example, the most successful of these rich surfaces, that of the Winslow house [figure 2]. Here the plain surface is first given a quiet, geometrical texture of balanced diagonals with inscribed circles and subordinate traceries, all quite as truly of the surface as upon it. From the main intersections of these are thrown outward and upward, crisp, virile, prickly leaf stalk, with their play of strong light and shade, quieted in turn by the conventionalized pendent spray of everlasting wisteria blossoms. An imaginative bit of tracery springs lightly forth from the common vertical axis of symmetry, enlivening the sober pendent and with its dainty sweep of opposition balancing the heavier flow of the bulkier leaves and completing a harmonious yet subtle rhythm. The Heller frieze, the figures of which were modelled by Richard Bock, lacks the exquisite repose of the Winslow detail, partly through an apparent miscalculation in the emphasis of relief upon the figures and the blossom pendents between them which spring from volute-like off-shoots of the conventional tracery which are relatively too weak. The idea, however, is as beautiful as it is novel and interesting, and a small section of this frieze cast in plaster and stained a deep wood-brown is effectively placed upon the great brick chimney in the Oak Park drawing-room.

In all of Mr. Wright's works the element of color plays its due part in the effect which they produce upon the beholder. He is a lover of rich, warm, quiet colors. Blues, cold greens and dead whites, except as incidentals, have no place in his color schemes. As an example of the care with which he chooses material for color and texture, the Winslow house will answer admirably. The softly mottled bricks range from a golden tan to a deep, ruddy orange, while the roof tiles were a special burning which produced an indescribable surface-tone approaching a soft salmon color. Frieze of dull tan, wood mouldings of brown, and eaves of golden yellow, throwing their reflected light into the upper casements, are the elements of the color scheme. The other buildings from his hand are less brilliant, but always quiet and unusually satisfactory in coloring which is managed to preserve the integrity of the larger masses of each composition. Affectation in manipulating materials for naive or unique effect is seldom found in his structures. The modern perfection of make and finish seem good enough and necessary to the best expression of the work.

Here, in this condensed monograph of a young man's work, a boy's work, perhaps, as he is but thirty-two, the best obtainable that he has done during an independent career of seven years has been concisely presented for the thoughtful consideration of the architects of America. No one more than he realizes and is grateful for the significance in this work of the early influence of Sullivan. Working together as master and trusted pupil for seven years, during a period of great undertakings, there must have been between two such ardent natures an interchange of thought and influence not wholly one-sided. To-day both are influencing in the same direction the enthusiastic youths who are taking up the burden of an architectural career in this free western atmosphere. Youth admires courage. Enthusiasm is contagious. Youth wants to be free and exults in the use of its own untrammeled power. As a leader of revolt against dead custom Frank Wright has come into touch with the younger spirits because of his own youth and because his work has varied from the humblest cottage to the largest project, because he has entered into every part of it with a zeal and courage which are a perpetual inspiration to those who understand and know him best.

In the Galleries (1907)

Harriet Monroe

After reading Harriet Monroe's review, Wright lamented to her that "praise isn't especially needed [but] I am hungry for the honest, genuine criticism that searches the soul of the thing." And well might he lament. She had said of his houses that they "show charm," and she dismissed his larger structures as "an interesting experiment. . . . at times even bizarre. . . . without grace or ease or monumental beauty."

Harriet Monroe was a midwesterner, a poet, and the biographer of Chicago architect John Root. She devoted much time to improving public comprehension of literature and the arts. On the occasion of the Chicago Architectural Club's annual exhibition in 1907 she reviewed it for the daily press. In her opening paragraphs she spoke of Wright, who was having his first major showing in five years.

One of the smaller galleries of those now devoted to the Architectural Club exhibition at the Art Institute is given over to the designs of Frank Lloyd Wright of Oak Park. There are many exhibits in this comprehensive group—beautiful drawings of dwellings, a church or two and an outdoor resort, and models for large buildings, specimens of glass, furniture, lamps, etc.

The Chicago *Examiner*, April 13, 1907.

Mr. Wright has cut loose from the schools and elaborated his own system of design. Like the art-nouveau enthusiasts abroad, he believes that the three Greek orders have done their utmost in the service of man, until in modern hands their true meaning is distorted and lost. Therefore he thinks it is time to discard them and all their renaissance derivatives, and begin afresh from the beginning. At least he believes such a rebirth to be the only course for him.

An Interesting Experiment
His work is thus a most interesting experiment, dependent for its success wholly upon the designer's creative force and in-born sense of architectural proportions and harmonies. The experiment has been worked out chiefly in the suburbs of Chi-cago, and is thus of special importance to us. Therefore this roomful of Mr. Wright's designs—so unusual, at times even bizarre—demands more than a questioning glance and a pass-ing word.

What is the measure of his success? His limitations are ob-vious enough. We pass by the more ambitious buildings—the plaster models for Unity Church at Oak Park, for the Larkin Company administration building at Buffalo, and for a huge, square nameless structure [Lincoln Center], all of which look too much like fantastic blockhouses, full of corners and angles and squat, square columns, massive and weighty, without grace or ease or monumental beauty [figures 5–10]. Mani-festly his imagination halts here; it labors and does not yet achieve beautiful and expressive buildings for public worship and business.

Dwellings Show Charm
But if at these two ends of the scale Mr. Wright's system of design seems inadequate to the strain imposed upon it, his dwellings, on the contrary, show its charm. Some of these low-browed, slant-roofed, unobtrusive houses, with groups of little windows and broad verandas nestling under the eaves, with gardens and walls and pergolas framing them in—some of these seem to grow out of the ground as naturally as the trees, and to express our hospitable suburban American life, a life of indoors and outdoors, as spontaneously as certain Ital-ian villas express the more pompous and splendid life of those old gorgeous centuries. Especially graceful in the grouping of

lines and masses are the dwellings of Avery Coonley at River-side, of Elizabeth Stone at Glencoe, of T. P. Hardy at Racine, and of V. H. Metsger away up on a rocky hill at Sault Ste. Marie.

The Larkin Building in Buffalo (1908)

Russell Sturgis

Sturgis was the foremost American architectural critic of his day, yet he could not abide the Larkin Building any more than John Ruskin, half a century earlier, could accept the Crystal Palace. From his nineteenth-century point of view it was not architecture because it lacked the rich, modulating ornament that he believed was essential to soften forms and enliven surface; it was "a monster of awkwardness. . . . an extremely ugly building" which he could condone only on utilitarian grounds. Although he sensed power in the design, he failed to comprehend the reason why.

Following the publication on the Larkin Building abroad, Buffalo became an essential stop for European architects on a visit to our shores. Few buildings in America were so revered and praised—and precisely for the reason that Sturgis had rejected it.

The Sturgis article, sometimes naively praised for its recognition of Wright, is very long. In the brief excerpts that follow I

Architectural Record 23, April 1908, pp. 311–321.

have endeavored to preserve its spirit while eliminating most

of the descriptive text.

The lover of architecture who looks at a building so entirely removed as this one from traditional styles feels a shock of surprise, and this surprise is the reverse of pleasant. Few persons who have seen the great monuments of the past will fail to pronounce this monument an extremely ugly building. It is, in fact, a monster of awkwardness, if we judge it by its lines and masses alone [figures 5–8].

One may try the experiment of familiarity to see whether with longer acquaintance the building is less ugly than it seems at the first look. Ruskin tells the story of his having been led astray by the theory of Use and Wont—by the notion that our liking for certain forms and colors is the result of familiarity, and nothing else, and he says that he kept a skull on his mantelpiece for months, but found it just as ugly when the months had passed. And so it is in all probability with this exterior. If we are to consider it as a piece of abstract form, as a thing which is itself ugly or the reverse, the opinion will remain fixed that nothing uglier could exist.

Suppose, for instance, that one who lived opposite this Larkin Building were to have his way for a month, and were to utilize his time in making the building less clumsy in his eyes— would he not begin by molding those square corners which are thrust upon us so sharply in all the exterior views, working those corners into upright beads and coves, developing, perhaps, in an angle shaft with capital and base?

Moldings are important and valuable, and the designer who rejects them altogether handicaps himself. But it is evident that the first principle laid down by the designer [of this building] for his own guidance was this—to avoid everything that would look like a merely architectural adornment, to add nothing for the sake of architectural effect. [Yet] you must add to a building something which is unnecessary, or you must have a bare, sharp-edged pile of blocks—a group of parallelopipedons like this. The designer seems to have said that even the rounding off of the coping shall be eschewed. He has determined that the square corner, the right angle, the straight edge, the sharp arris, the firm vertical and horizontal lines, unbroken, unmodified, uncompromizing in their geometrical precision—that these and these only shall be the features of his building. But as that characteristic of the building prevents it from having any delicate light and shade, therefore it stands condemned in the eyes of any person who looks at the building asking for beauty of effect.

If, now, we seek to take up a sympathetic position, to consider the building as perhaps the architect himself considered it, there are to notice the care given to the plan and disposition of the halls and rooms, the care which has evidently resulted in a successful utilitarian building. Construction which is the simplest and most obvious, and which cannot go astray because everything is reduced to the post and lintel; workmanship which is faultless, simple and straightforward brickwork; piers and walls fairly and smoothly built—all these things unite to make a building which no one can fail to accept. And while everything has been carried out with a view to practical utility, there has been also some attempt to adorn, to beautify. But we have already seen reason to think that this attempt has failed.

An Architectural Pioneer: Review of the Portfolios Containing the Works of Frank Lloyd Wright (1912)

Montgomery Schuyler

Sturgis judged Wright using Ruskin's standards while Schuyler followed the rationalist approach of Viollet-le-Duc and obviously fared much better. Yet finally he too rejects Wright's designs for their lack of ornament. To him they seem unfinished. He says "The stark unmodelled transitions give an air of something rude, incomplete, unfinished. The buildings seem 'blocked out' and awaiting completion rather than completed."

Sturgis and Schuyler were the two most distinguished architectural critics in America in their day, and it is understandable why Wright became antagonistic toward those who professed competence to assess his work.

Schuyler reviews Ausgeführte Bauten und Entwürfe von Frank Lloyd Wright, *that magnificent folio of one hundred drawings, details, and plans published in 1910 by Ernst Wasmuth of Berlin. The long introductory text, which detracts from the value of the whole, discusses various historical and contemporary*

Architectural Record 31, April 1912, pp. 427–436.

styles of architecture as a basis for judging Wright. Only the

final paragraphs of this review are reprinted here.

What all the designs illustrated in these two portfolios show is an attempt at the organic, an attempt to organize the requirements of the given building into a whole made up of related and interdependent parts, to find the seed, so to say, in order to grow the flower. Every one of them, whatever else may be said about it, is a growth and not a compilation. Every one of them shows that power of simplification and unification which was the essential gift of Richardson, and which was quite independent of his fondness for Romanesque detail, for exaggerated voussoirs and dwarfed columns. The simplicity of the ground plan is always noticeable. Mr. Ashbee calls it "noble" and we will not quarrel with his adjective. The prevailing horizontality Mr. Wright claims to be especially "domestic." For that matter, it happens to be quite in accordance with the current fashion in domestic architecture, in works which have nothing else in common with these. It may also have, as he further maintains, some special congruity with what Lowell describes as

Broad prairie rather, genial, level-lined,
Fruitful and friendly for all human kind;
Yet also nigh to heaven and loved of loftiest stars.

In times and countries in which architecture is a living art, the general form of building corresponds to the environment, and the bristling pyramid of the Abbey of Mont St. Michel would be as impossible in the midst of the Roman Campagna or of an Illinois prairie as the spreading expanse of the temple of Karnak on the spike of the Mont itself. Fitness is part of the dignity of these elevations, which in the best examples is undoubtedly great. But what makes the real impressiveness of these designs is that they are organic wholes, that the variety of their parts, without being denied or slurred, is overruled into an effective unity, that they are not compiled out of picturesque "bits" which have caught the eye of the designer in a rapid tour, or in a still more rapid rummage through a pile of photographs.

The defect of their quality will be evident to every practiced inspector. Those functional modifications of surface or of line, commonly by means of mouldings, to form a footing, to emphasize a division, to soften or to sharpen a transition, to mark a projection or a recess, which have been employed in every artistic mode of building from the Egyptian downward, are here almost altogether absent, nor can their place be supplied, as to the artistic result, by decoration strictly and properly so called. The defect of the architecture is the same as the defect of the "Mission" furniture, which it appears that the architect commonly, and properly, specifies to go with it. The stark unmodelled transitions give an air of something rude, incomplete, unfinished. The buildings seem "blocked out," and awaiting completion rather than completed. The lack is nothing at all against the theory of design in the author's mind, nothing against the reduction of the theory to practice so far as it has gone. It is a deficiency which belongs to an art in its lusty youth rather than in its decadence, and indeed we can find it in the early Romanesque, which was a living style if ever there was one, in comparison with its own later phase, and still more in comparison with the developed Gothic. Moreover, it is a deficiency which can be supplied and will be supplied, when it is once recognized that the mode of design to which it is not a necessary drawback has "the promise and potency of life." A pioneer must have patience and so indeed must those who believe in him. He should be willing to say with Bacon: "I could not be true and constant to this argument I handle if I were not willing to go beyond others, yet not more willing than to have others go beyond me." Meanwhile, it is hard to see how an unprejudiced inquirer can deny that such designers as Mr. Sullivan and Mr. Wright have the root of the matter, and that their works are of good hope, in contrast with the rehandling and rehashing of admired historical forms in which there is no future nor any possibility of progress.

A Comparison of Master and Pupil Seen in Two Houses (1911)

Anonymous

The Architectural Record, *which deserves an accolade for its unswerving faith in Wright, published a study in 1911 entitled "Two Unusual Houses by Louis Sullivan and Frank Lloyd Wright." While not a thorough account, the article offered a sympathetic discussion of Sullivan's Babson house and Wright's subsequently famous Coonley house, both just completed at Riverside, Illinois. However the* Western Architect *of Minneapolis, in keeping with its obvious distaste for Wright, summarized the* Architectural Record *article in a front-page report that was fallacious and completely biased—and evidently written for no other reason than to slander Wright.*

In a series of comparative illustrations, the *Architectural Record* presents two houses recently completed in Oak Park [*sic*, Riverside] and in the same neighborhood with the same general landscape surroundings. One is the work of Louis H. Sullivan and the other that of his erstwhile pupil, Frank Lloyd Wright. In the description of these houses accompanying the illustrations, the writer is as kind to Mr. Wright as he can well be and as analytically just to Mr. Sullivan as the "invidious comparison" will allow. He does not say so in words, but in effect, that the house by Mr. Wright, while startlingly beautiful as a sketch, is practically a freak in its livable quality, while that by Mr. Sullivan bears out that architect's theory of natural growth from inherent purpose in design. . . .

Western Architect 17, November 1911, p. 95.

None have gone so far into the realm of the picturesque, or failed so signally in the production of livable houses as Frank Lloyd Wright. When the architectural history of this generation is written, his name will be mentioned as one who saw a light in the direction of a national style in design but failed to understand the direction by which it must be reached.

Part IV

European Discovery (1910–1930s)

By 1912, European architects knew of Wright's designs
through American and foreign journals, from the publications
of Ernst Wasmuth and, increasingly, from personal visits to the
United States. To many, and especially the younger generation
of Dutch and German designers, his work came as a breath of
spring. The timing was perfect for those men who soon were
to formulate such important movements as the Amsterdam
School, de Stijl, German Expressionism, and the International
Style. Some responded to Wright's revolutionary concept of
defining space—which utilized planes and masses rather than
enclosing walls. Others were inspired by the latent expressionism of his forms—as at Unity Temple and the Larkin Building. Still others admired the monumental simplicity of his
designs—where ordered shapes and natural textures replaced
the traditional need for ornament: Wright had created classic
monumentality without resort to Classicism. And in Holland,
where brick was the major element in construction, Wright's
handling of this material remained a constant source of inspiration.

This European interest in Wright produced a spate of publications. Those written in the teens and twenties were by architects while those published later were more often by critics and historians. A selection is reprinted here. There are additional publications worth mentioning, including a discussion of Wright and American architecture by Werner Moser (Das Werk, *May 1925), and by Herman Sörgel (Baukunst, February 1926)—with the same issue containing contributions by Barry Byrne (Wright's former apprentice) and Eric Mendelsohn.*

Mendelsohn also evaluated Wright's historical significance in Das Neue Berlin *(September 1929) and prepared a general appreciation for* Wendingen *in 1925. This Dutch periodical (representing the group known as the Amsterdam School) dedicated seven special issues to Wright in 1925. Included were articles by H. P. Berlage, J. J. P. Oud, Th. Wijdeveld (the editor), Mendelsohn, Maillet-Stevens, Lewis Mumford, and Wright. When complete, the series was bound and issued as a book,* The Life-Work of the American Architect Frank Lloyd Wright. *In addition, a new edition of the Wasmuth folio came out in 1924, and H. de Fries' study in German was published in 1926. In France meanwhile, "Cahiers d'art" published a little book in 1928 by the American historian Henry-Russell Hitchcock and in 1930 L'Architecture Vivante devoted a monograph issue to Wright's work. Yet no book on Wright was published in America until 1942—thirty-two years after the first one appeared abroad!*

European Discovery (1910–1930s)

*By the 1930s Europeans began to assess the prodigious impact that Wright had made upon them. Mendelsohn broached the subject in 1929, Catherine Bauer considered it in 1931 (*New Republic, *June 24, 1931) and Nikolaus Pevsner analyzed it in 1939 (*Architects' Journal, *May 4, 1939). Not until after the second World War did Americans start writing about this subject.*

A Tribute to Frank Lloyd Wright (1910/1946)

Mies van der Rohe

Mies van der Rohe was generous in acknowledging his debt to others. Here he speaks of the profound and salutary influence that Wright had upon him and other Europeans when they first learned of his work through the Wasmuth publications and the Berlin exhibition of 1910.

We young architects found ourselves in painful inner conflict. We were ready to pledge ourselves to an idea. But the potential vitality of the architectural idea of this period had, by that time, been lost.

This, then, was the situation in 1910.

At this moment, so critical for us, there came to Berlin the exhibition of the work of Frank Lloyd Wright. This comprehensive display and the extensive publication of his works enabled us really to become acquainted with the achievement of this architect. The encounter was destined to prove of great significance to the development of architecture in Europe.

The work of this great master revealed an architectural world of unexpected force and clarity of language, and also a disconcerting richness of form. Here finally was a master-builder drawing upon the veritable fountainhead of architecture, who with true originality lifted his architectural creations into the light. Here, again, at last, genuine organic architecture flowered.

College Art Journal 6, Autumn 1946, pp. 41–42.
Reprinted by permission, College Art Association.

The more deeply we studied Wright's creations, the greater became our admiration for his incomparable talent, for the boldness of his conceptions, and for his independence in thought and action. The dynamic impulse emanating from his work invigorated a whole generation. His influence was strongly felt even when it was not actually visible.

After this first encounter, we followed the development of this rare man with eager hearts. We watched with astonishment the exuberant unfolding of the gifts of one who had been endowed by nature with the most splendid talents. In his undiminishing power he resembles a giant tree in a wide landscape, which, year after year, ever attains a more noble crown.

The New American Architecture (1912)

H. P. Berlage

H. P. Berlage, famed architect of the Amsterdam Bourse
(1898–1900), was revered by the younger generation in Eu-
rope as one of the founders of the modern movement. He was
a rationalist, greatly concerned with logical expression of
structure and the nature of materials. In 1911 he visited
America intent upon seeing the work of Sullivan and Wright,
and after returning home lectured extensively—not just in
Holland but in Germany and Switzerland as well. Because of
these lectures Le Corbusier learned of Wright, and anyone
who now visits Amsterdam, Hilversum, or other Dutch cities is
well aware of Wright's profound influence there.

To Berlage must go credit for first articulating Wright's contri-
bution to the design of interior space. He also speaks of the
restfulness and the sense of quiet repose which these interiors
create, and he describes them as being "plastic" rather than
two dimensional. In his opinion the Larkin Building was
Wright's masterpiece, an assessment quite opposite from that
of Russell Sturgis (see page 115).

Schweizerische Bauzeitung 60, September 14, 1912, pp. 148–150; September 21, 1912, pp. 165–167.

On March 30, 1912, Berlage presented a slide lecture on Sullivan and Wright to the Zurich Association of Engineers and Architects. He summarized his statements for the Schweizerische Bauzeitung *and the text, rather rough and hastily written, is much abridged here.*

Frank Lloyd Wright studied under Sullivan and, like his mentor, his designs retain nothing that reminds us of historical styles. His is an original architecture. He works to simplify architectural masses, while treating ornament as something purely secondary. His forms are so original that in the final analysis no contemporary European tendencies are visible in his work.

Wright specializes in the design of country houses, of which the D. D. Martin house is typical [figures 3–4]. It has only two floors with the ground floor extending in a horizontal sequence of spaces because all of the rooms open into one another. Americans do not necessarily close off the living areas of a house with doors, although occasionally they screen the openings with curtains. As a result one has beautiful views throughout the interior, not only from room to room but also from the various rooms into the hall and staircase. These effects are heightened because Americans are adept at decorating their houses with objects of art. Wright, being fond of flowers, occasionally extends a wall out from under a window in order to create a trench or box in which flowers can be planted. The view, out over the flowers and into the garden, is sensational.

The low pitched roof, in an unexpected manner, rests directly on top of the upper story, and many of these rooms have the underside of the roof as their ceiling. This, combined with generously projecting eaves, imparts to the room an amazingly quiet tone. Such a house is extremely attractive. It gives the impression of extraordinary intimacy, and it was only with great difficulty that I departed from these splendid rooms. Their originality is best described as "plastic"—in contrast to European interiors which are flat and two-dimensional. Both

inside and out one recognizes the originality of these homes—
an originality that permits us to speak of a new, indigenous
American architecture since there is nothing comparable to it
in Europe.

Having been told that Wright's masterpiece was the Larkin
Company office building in Buffalo, New York, I went to see it
and must confess that this is an understatement [figures 5–8].
The building consists of only one large room, thanks to the
American concept that offices should not be divided into separate rooms. The head of the office works at the same table as
his employees, and from his table his view encompasses the
entire room with its various floors which, like galleries, sur-
round the central hall. This hall has excellent light in spite of
the large brick masses that form the exterior corner towers;
indeed, the effect is similar to Unity Temple where the corner
staircases are lighted from inside.

The building is conceived in terms of contrasting masses—
and these have a very powerful effect. Whatever may be one's
concept of an office, particularly here in Europe, I assure you
that there is no building here with the monumental power of
this American design. The exterior and interior are both of
brick, with floors and ceilings of concrete. Detailing is handled
naturally, in accordance with Wright's originality, and clearly
shows his creative genius.

I left convinced that I had seen a great modern work, and I am
filled with respect for the master who created a design that is
without equal in the whole of Europe.

During the trip I looked primarily at the work of Sullivan and
Wright . . . the two greatest American architects of our time.
And when I left I was convinced that a new architecture is
being created there. We Europeans have no reason to regard
American architecture as inferior. On the contrary, the best
work demonstrates both originality and imagination, and
promises much for the future. We should accord it the high
estimation that it so richly deserves.

Architectural Observations Concerning Wright and the Robie House (1918)

J. J. P. Oud

J. J. P. Oud, one of the foremost Dutch architects of his day, is linked through his work to several of the modern movements—including early in his career the Amsterdam School, and soon after (as they evolved) to de Stijl and the International Style. This short article appeared in volume one of De Stijl, *the journal that gave its name to the movement with which the painter Mondrian is inexorably identified.*

Oud compares Wright's work to subsequent developments in European painting, specifically to Futurism, but also to Cubism which he details in a 1925 article—and he might have included de Stijl as well. He also discusses Wright's floor plans, and the art of pure proportions, which is what Europeans so much admired at the Larkin Building.

The article appears here for the first time in English.

In the Robie house [1907–1909, figures 11–12] we see a new departure from architectural design as we have previously known it. The embellishment of the building (which here in Holland is nearly always attempted by the secondary means of detail—ornament), is here achieved by primary means: the

De Stijl 1, no. 4, 1918, pp. 39–41. Translated by Elsa Scharbach.

effect of the masses themselves. Instead of a stable and rigid compactness of the various parts, Wright *detaches the masses from the whole* and rearranges their composition. There is a direct relation here with the way the futurists have overcome rigidity in painting—which is by achieving movement of the planes. In this way Wright has created a new "plastic" architecture. His masses slide back and forth and left and right; there are plastic effects in all directions. This movement, which one finds in his work, opens up entirely new aesthetic possibilities for architecture. Such a concern is considerably more impressive and modern than is the use of detail by means of which our own modern architecture, known as the Amsterdam School, endeavors to find expression.

The effect that Wright achieves in the Robie house is partly due to his highly appropriate use of reinforced concrete, as seen in the long terrace. This expression is not absolutely pure, however, because brick conceals the concrete—with the result that the concrete shows its essence but not its characteristic appearance. Yet the function of reinforced concrete is clearly stated since such a span, made in such a way, cannot be conceived in any other material.

In this house one completely feels the spirit of our age. One obtains a similar impression from a moving locomotive. One thinks of an automobile, rather than a horse-drawn carriage, as being appropriate for this home.

All parts of the building, as well as the furniture, have been manufactured by machine. The construction of this, and all great modern buildings, is different from earlier buildings because today's architect is not continually present on the site but visits it only for inspection. He directs construction from his office and it is there that he sets down the forms and the proportions which are executed by others. Thus modern architecture is becoming more and more a question of proportions, and in this it corresponds with modern painting. But the creation of an architecture based solely on proportions, so striking in some of Wright's other work, has not reached its fullest expression in the Robie house.

Wright's ground plans are an endless source of aesthetic joy to the experienced critic. Their composition is clear and uncluttered, and the proportions and arrangement of spaces, individually and collectively, is faultlessly determined. The practical function of the house—its purpose—is the basis of the plan, and the basic concept is evident in the way the practical means have been applied. No little bay windows here, no little annexes or sensational effects. And whatever ornament has been applied is absorbed into the whole by the large, protecting roof.

Frank Lloyd Wright (1921)

Jan Wils

This insightful essay, made available for the first time in English, clearly states which values the Europeans saw as the most significant in Wright's work, and as such stands in sharp contrast to the American writings that we have already read. Some of the themes touched on here were treated earlier by Berlage and Oud, yet these subjects are more completely developed and elucidated in the present, abridged, text. Jan Wils was a practicing Dutch architect whose own career was profoundly influenced by Wright.

The quotations in the text are generally from Wright's 1908 article, "In the Cause of Architecture."

Walt Whitman is the man who in his "Song of the Open Road" has described the new society. Frank Lloyd Wright has opened the way for the new architecture. These two men have laid the cornerstone for the buildings of the future.

Even as Walt Whitman saw world events in one wide vision and wrote his poems accordingly, so Wright saw the change effected on society by the introduction of steam and electricity and designed his buildings correspondingly. He saw that our little houses made it impossible to relax in a life lived ten times faster; that our little houses with all their little corridors

Elsevier's Geïllustreerd Maandschrift 61, no. 4, 1921, pp. 217–227. Amsterdam. Translated by Elsa Scharbach.

and little compartments did not fit together "like a machine", but that they lacked clarity and cost enormous sums to maintain. Openness, lucidity, and the concentration of related activities are the basis of his ground plans. "Simplicity and Repose are qualities that measure the true value of any work of art." One consequence of this is that a building should contain as few rooms as possible, and the architect should try to simplify them. One room is actually sufficient if separated from the service area by "architectural contrivances."

Something else strikes us in Wright's ground plans.

America is the country where the principle of democracy is inborn in every citizen. Equal rights for all is the rule. This implies a respect for oneself—which we often take for arrogance but which in fact is a valid trait. A home-owner wants to see respect for himself expressed in his house; he wants to live his own life, undisturbed by others' interests. When he withdraws from the hustle and bustle of daily life, he wants to be able to retire to a place where he is not bothered by servants or the indiscreet eyes of strangers.

In the ground plan lies the true modernity of Wright's architecture.

Throughout the centuries each change in lifestyle appeared first in the ground plan of the house, and this change in plan produced a different type of exterior design. Historians are mistaken when they observe only these outer changes, and consider the plan to be a consequence of them. The studies of Viollet-le-Duc and later Muthesius, in *Das Englische Haus*, have demonstrated that the ground plan is primary, and that the exterior design is the result.

Therefore if there is to be a modern architecture, there will have to be a complete revolution in the ground plan of buildings—resulting from our change in lifestyle. Any other external changes, which are only external and do not affect the interior, are not modern and can only lead us to a dead end.

Wright has realized his conceptions by using the materials of his time. Iron, reinforced concrete, seamless constructions, central heating, and the ample use of electricity enable him to solve the problems put before him. In the application of these

European Discovery (1910–1930s)

materials he has not begun by asking "what is the most peculiar peculiarity of the material?" but rather "what is its true character?"

In his appreciation for new materials Wright has never rejected the old, well-known ones. The new he complements with the qualities of the old, and with fine judgment combines all of them according to their greatest value into a pure harmonic whole. "Bring out the nature of the materials, let their nature intimately into your scheme. Strip the wood of varnish and let it alone—stain it. Develop the natural texture of the plastering and stain it. No treatment can be really a matter of fine art, when the natural characteristics are, or their nature is, outraged or neglected."

Wood, brick, slate, tile, marble cannot be replaced, in their various qualities, by a new material. It is their application which is subject to change. The material is a means, a means to express a state of soul, a state of soul closely related to a new concept of life, a concept of life greatly influenced by new events. Thus the application of the old materials will be a function of the introduction of machines. "The machine is the normal tool of our civilization, give it work that it can do well; nothing is of greater importance. To do this will be to formulate new industrial ideals, sadly needed."

In designing the exterior of his houses Wright uses the same point of departure as in his ground plans, that is, each part is molded and formed into a shape corresponding to its function in the whole. Then all these loose pieces are assembled, and with a masterly touch he combines them into an architectural whole. The idea of architecture is expressed more strongly here than anywhere else. Architecture does not mean looking at a facade as a flat surface and by means of ornamentation making a tasteful composition, but architecture is the grouping of masses; these masses are the various organs of the house, the rooms, the necessary spaces. The architect acts as creator by making chaotic confusion into an organic whole. Architecture is not an art of planes but of spaces; that is to say the masses can be shown on a plane in the ground plan, but have to express themselves in space as single masses in a logical relationship with each other, in a rhythmic alternation of high and low, light and dark.

When viewing Wright's houses one has to remember that they were designed for the prairies, those rolling or flat planes of the West, where any change in elevation is exceptional, where each tree rises like a tower above that great flowered tapestry and under that magnificent sky. The solution is not easy. Yet Wright has succeeded in finding one. His buildings are wide, low, and long. Each interior space shows its true proportions on the outside and this composition of various parts is covered by a flat roof which often protrudes far out over the facade. Wide, heavy bands accentuate the horizontal effect of the building, while the rising lines of chimneys, and sometimes also of windows, are the only contrast to this horizontal effect. But those horizontal lines, along terraces and garden walls, give an impression of movement—one feels a close relationship with modern means of transportation for example—but they also give an impression of restfulness; there is a complete static balance and at the same time a sublime repose.

In a few buildings Wright has sought balance in a different way, namely by strongly expressing the functions of support and supported. In these designs the corner pillars stand as heavy massive supports for the roof. Between these pillars the floors are strung, and these reinforced concrete constructions hold up the parapets. Sometimes the floors protrude for several meters, forming balconies which cantilever from the wall without any visible form of support. To our minds, still used to old construction methods, these far-protruding unsupported conceptions seem strange, but they are immediately acceptable when we remember what reinforced concrete is.

Two buildings deserve our special attention. They are Unity Temple and the office building of the Larkin Company [figures 5–10]. Except for these two structures, Wright has not yet had an opportunity to design public buildings. Nevertheless these examples prove that he can create the great monument of our time.

Again it is the function which determines the plan. In the office building the ground plan was determined by the concept of the enterprise, by the need for easy control from each part of the building, and by the requirement to have all the employees together yet at a certain distance from each other. And the church was conceived as a gathering place for a group of people, who in strict separation from the world, want to concentrate for some time on a different thought.

The forms which Wright conceived are utterly simple, but in their simplicity they give an impression of the greatest monumentality possible.

The ground plan of the Larkin Building is very simple in its arrangement. There is an inner court, around which the several stories are laid out, being held up by piers which go from the floor to the roof. Daylight enters through a skylight over the inner court, and through windows between the piers on the outer wall. Next to the main building one finds an auxiliary structure containing such services as toilets, wardrobes, etc. On the top floor of the main building there is a lunchroom along with everything needed to keep people occupied between working hours. And on top of that there is a wintergarden as well as a roofgarden.

The various parts of the building are clearly expressed on the outside. Just as in Wright's houses, each part is separate from the others. Like two strong anchors the stairwells hold the core (the stairs are lit by small skylights at a right angle with the flights, in order to avoid facing the light when mounting). Between the stairwells the big inner court extends forward, with the piers extending still further in order to support the unbroken space of the kitchen on the top floor. At the side it is the length of the inner court which is expressed. The parapets are simply strung between the piers. The stairwells close off the corners.

This entire composition is so simple and so logical that no further description or explanation is needed. One sees it, and one senses the tempo of our time; it is here that the spirit of creativity is at its highest, where system and order form the basis of the enterprise, and where, in spite of the high demands made on the employees, their material interests have not been overlooked and everything possible has been done to provide for work, as well as for rest and recreation.

And so this building radiates strength, not only because of the large size of all the planes and masses, but even more because of the monumental proportions. Just as nothing on the inside was left to whim, so on the outside there are no complicating elements; the same clarity of movement is found inside and out. The businesslike spirit, the inner strength of the building, gives it an outward appearance which places it on a level with the great architectural monuments of the past, but to us it has a higher value because it is a monument of our time.

Of no less importance is Unity Temple [figures 9–10]. The concept of this building is similar to the office building we have just discussed. A square space, the gathering place for the audience, is surrounded by a gallery and once again the stairs are in the corners of the building. The building stands as if held in place by the four stair towers, yet it rises high above them and pushes, as it were, the galleries out to the sides. Flat roofs cover each of these parts, protruding where necessary, as above the windows. The solution for the windows is very remarkable, and at the same time of unprecedented beauty. This building, more than any other, shows that the window is not a necessary evil but the natural ornament of the facade. Simple little piers stand on the high parapet, supporting the flat roof; the openings between the piers are filled with glass—that is the basic system of construction. Yet, how great is the effect, how mighty is the repose of the horizontal parapet between the vertical planes of the stairtowers, how simple and obvious is the support of the slab roof, and how controlled is the detail and the grouping of the masses. This is pure architecture; this is true building when each material and each element in the mass relates to the whole, and everything is carefully studied and composed. This construction is as clear as the human body, in which the function of each part is expressed.

The Unity Temple is constructed of concrete. Not by the usual method of reinforcement, but cast. After the form-work was dismantled, the surface was brushed in order to show its texture, its composition. As a monolith this monument to our time stands in Oak Park, a true milestone in the history of architecture.

We have intentionally discussed these two buildings more extensively than Wright's houses. Important as his dwellings are, with their emphasis on the essential function and the well-considered use of materials, they are not completely free from some romanticism. In the Larkin Building and Unity Temple this element is completely lacking and the architect has achieved the highest degree of purity. Therefore their greater value.

Part V

More Recent Evaluation

Finally, after almost three decades of neglect, interest in Wright's architecture began to revive in America during the late thirties and forties. Earlier, in the twenties, when a spate of books on the history of American architecture appeared by such writers as Edgell, Hamlin, Kimball, Mumford, and Tallmadge, Wright was usually ignored or mentioned only in some derogatory way. Kimball, alone, accorded him worthy recognition, while Tallmadge, Wright's erstwhile colleague, labeled him a 'has been' and included his work in a chapter entitled "Louis Sullivan and the Lost Cause."

Attitudes changed, however, and by 1941 New York's Museum of Modern Art sponsored a Frank Lloyd Wright exhibition in conjunction with which Henry-Russell Hitchcock published his classic work, In the Nature of Materials, the first book about Wright to appear in English. Thereafter, with very gradually increasing frequency, came the eventual deluge of articles and books of more recent years. Selections from this rich variety of material are to be found in parts I and II, with other examples reprinted here.

Frank Lloyd Wright and the New Pioneers (1929)

Lewis Mumford

Earlier remarks about the lack of perceptive comment on Wright in America between 1901 and the 1940s admit to one remarkable exception—the writings of Lewis Mumford. As early as 1929 he penned this timeless review which touches not only upon the essence of Wright's creative genius but squarely tackles that contentious question of architecture versus the industrial age—an issue he resolves in favor of Wright over those younger Europeans who professed to create a machine-age art.

Hitchcock, whose youthful booklet inspired this review, subsequently became the dean of American architectural historians and our great authority on Wright.

This monograph on Frank Lloyd Wright has the honor of being the first of a series on the masters of contemporary architecture; and, as everyone knows who is familiar with the history of modern architecture in America and Europe, the honor is well-deserved. The writer, however, is not a Frenchman, but an American, Mr. Henry-Russell Hitchcock [whose] introduction occupies only four pages of this monograph, the rest con-

Architectural Record 65, April 1929, pp. 414–416 (Review of Henry-Russell Hitchcock's *Frank Lloyd Wright*, Collection "Les Maîtres de l'Architecture Contemporaine," Editions "Cahiers d'Art," Paris, 1928)
Courtesy of *Architectural Record*.

sisting chiefly of photographs of Mr. Wright's buildings, together with a few obscurely reproduced plans; yet in these four pages Mr. Hitchcock manages to raise, by statement or implication, many of the important issues that must be faced in modern architecture.

To begin at the beginning, Mr. Hitchcock places Mr. Wright at the head of the movement which is represented by Berlage in Holland and by Hoffmann in Austria. This manner of placing Mr. Wright puts him definitely with the past generation, and it serves to bring out Mr. Hitchcock's underlying thesis of a cleavage in form between the generation of Wright and the generation of Le Corbusier and Oud, but it ignores the fact that America has gone through a different architectural and social development from Europe, and that the contemporaries of Berlage and Hoffmann, architecturally speaking, are Richardson and Sullivan. The worship of industrialism, which has become the keynote of the modern movement in Europe today, belongs to an earlier generation in America, that which actually built the grain elevators and the primitive skyscrapers of Chicago. There is, of course, a difference in technical methods between a stone construction like the Monadnock Building and a house by Le Corbusier but the philosophy and method of approach are exactly the same.

This limitation of architectural design to its technical elements was native in America; but it was none the less thoroughgoing; and the buildings that it produced are still, in their rigorous line and bold mass, among the best we can show: if they lack much that architecture can give, everything they do possess is a clean gain. When Mr. Hitchcock observes that Mr. Wright has learned less from the "lesson of Ford" than the European has, he neglects the fact that the Chicago of Mr. Wright's youth was wholly conceived in the image of Ford; business success and mechanical efficiency were the only factors that entered into the architectural problem; and Mr. Wright's development, instead of being toward the goal of the "building-machine" had this conception, rather, as a starting point.

Had the Chicago architects of the eighties been as intellectually conscious as Le Corbusier, and had they had an intelligent public, ready to apply in the home the successes they could boast of in the office building, there would have been dwelling houses which reflected all the virtues that the "new pioneers" seek to enthrone. The victory of the new pioneers in Chicago was incomplete, partly because of their failure to organize their gains, and partly because, in the hands of Sullivan and Wright, their architecture began to go through a natural and inevitable process of development. With his fundamental education as an engineer, and with that solid acquaintance with utilitarian necessities which the very being of Chicago gives, to a philosopher like Dewey or to a poet like Sandburg quite as much as to the businessman or industrialist, Mr. Wright took the next step. This step consisted in the modification of mechanical forms in harmony with the regional environment and with human desires and feelings.

Here is the point where Mr. Hitchcock's admiration suddenly wilts. He sees in Mr. Wright's use of ornament partly the pressure of rich clients, partly the "bad influence" of Sullivan, and partly Mr. Wright's own concern for the picturesque. Instead of becoming harder and harder in line, starker and starker, bleaker and bleaker, Mr. Wright's art became more rich and warm. In the Imperial Hotel in Tokyo Mr. Wright—forced to design for a people with habits of work other than those of the West—even embraced handicraft and permitted the building to take on the complicated forms of craftsmanship, the result being a monument far less European and mechanical than the painful sub-European specimens of architecture which the native architects scatter over the East. There is more ornament in the Imperial Hotel, 1916, or the Millard Residence in Pasadena, 1923, than in the Willits house, 1901. If Mr. Hitchcock is right, this phase of Mr. Wright's development is an unfortunate atavism; and it makes more and more pronounced the breach between his work and that which will be produced during the coming generation.

That is one view of the case, but my own belief is just the opposite of this. The glorification of the machine by people who are just becoming acquainted with its possibilities and are learning to use it is "modern" in Europe today precisely because it is forty years behind our American experience. While for Europe the lesson of Ford is increasing standardization and mass-production, because few of the economies in design so introduced have been practised there, for us the lesson of Ford which he learned at a price that would have bankrupted an ordinary manufacturer is the pathetic insufficiency of our old-fashioned industrial design, with its contempt for problems of pure form and its disregard for other human interests than efficiency. If this be true, Mr. Wright is not the forerunner of Le Corbusier but, in a real sense, his successor. He has passed that painful step in learning when one is conscious of one's movements and one's instruments, and has reached that period in pure mechanical design when he can play with it; in short, the engineer has given way to the artist, and despite a hundred efforts to prove either that the engineer *is* the artist, or that engineering is the only possible type of art in the modern world, Mr. Wright's work exists as a living refutation of this notion. He had achieved Cubism in architecture before the Cubists; and he has gone on to an integral architecture which creates its own forms with—not for—the machine.

Mr. Hitchcock's aesthetic and social philosophy keep him, I think, from recognizing this as a valid development; hence his disparagement of Mr. Wright's art at the very moment he is seeking to praise it. For me, on the contrary, Mr. Wright's architectural development justifies itself; and not the less so, certainly, because I am more interested in humanity and its needs and desires than I am in the abstract perfection of the machine, or in the pragmatic justification of Spengler's historical dogmas.

In failing to grasp the inevitability of this humanization of the machine, this addition of feeling to form, or of poetry to mathematics as we become more and more the master of it, Mr. Hitchcock has, it seems to me, lost the central clue in Mr. Wright's career. This becomes apparent in the final apostrophe, in which he compares him with Wren and repeats the phrase so true of Wren in the city of London: "si monumentum requiris circumspice." The comparison does not hold at any point; but it falls down chiefly on the mere historical detail that one cannot find Wright's work by looking around one in Chicago; on the contrary, one must search and pry and go on long motor rides, only to find, as in the Midway Gardens—built but fifteen years ago—that vandals have already ruined the building. Up to recently Mr. Wright had built no skyscrapers, and with all the vast volume of industrial and semi-industrial building he has had little to do. His architecture is not in the current of the present regime any more than Walt Whitman's writings were in the current of the Gilded Age: hence his value is not that he has dominated the scene and made it over in his image, but that he has kept the way open for a type of architecture which can come into existence only in a much more humanized and socially adept generation than our own.

Mr. Wright's art is prophetic: it does not simply conform and adjust itself to existing conditions; it reacts and makes demands; demands that the builder of speculative houses or rent-barracks has no intention of complying with. Success under present conditions demands unhesitating conformity on the part of the engineer to the terms laid down by the banker and investor; the result is sometimes good design and economy, and quite as often it is poor design and deformity and inadequacy to perform the function that the building is supposed to perform. This is not the milieu in which good architecture can become the rule, and if modern architecture flourishes in Europe and lags here, it is because the Europeans have far better conditions under which to work, as a result of the socialized activity of European municipalities, with their comprehensive and financially unremunerative housing programs.

The truth is that Mr. Wright's capital qualities alienate him both from the architects who do not acknowledge a handicap in conforming to the present demands and from the society that ignores the higher values of life if they happen to conflict with the principle of a quick turnover and a maximum profit. Chief among these qualities is Mr. Wright's sense of the natural environment; and here again, I think, Mr. Hitchcock's principles keep him from grasping Mr. Wright's significance. Mr. Hitchcock refers to the "absurdity and the provincialism of the term prairie architecture" to characterize Mr. Wright's early Chicago work. On the contrary, the phrase is not absurd but accurate. Mr. Wright is, definitely, our greatest regional architect; his Chicago houses *are* prairie houses, as his Pasadena houses are "mediterranean" ones, to harmonize with that climate and milieu. Even machines, as some of our new pioneers forget, differ in design according to the region they are used in: steamers designed for tropical trade have larger ventilating units than the usual North Atlantic liners, and automobiles in England are designed for low power because of the relatively easy contours of the country. The essential form of architecture is of course largely conditioned by the method of construction; but this again is not independent of regional qualifications—as the use of the concrete form instead of the steel frame in Chicago testifies.

Now, these qualities were largely ignored by the older classical architecture, with its concern for a single method of construction and a single mode of design. Wherever a building was placed or whatever its purpose, the problem of the architect was to make it resemble, as far as possible, a Greek or Roman temple. The neo-classicists of the machine have revamped this formula, but the spirit behind it is the same; the chief difference being that the archetypal form is no longer a temple but a factory, and the principal offense against taste consists, not in the use of free or "barbarous" ornament but in the use of any ornament at all, however integral, however intimately a part of the design and necessary for its completion. Mr. Wright's great virtue consists in the fact that he uses to the full modern methods of construction and boldly invents new forms without losing his great sense of tact—the tact of the artist with his materials, of the lover of nature with the earth, and of a man with other men. Hence the importance of the garden which surrounds and completes almost all of his buildings: it is a true symbol of his entire work—the picture of life, warm, earthy, insurgent, breaking in waves of foliage over the stony masses of the building, and showing the power and logic of the form at the very moment of departing from it and counterbalancing it. This is an art which cannot be contained in a narrow classical formula; and if the new pioneers have as yet no place for it in their philosophy, so much the worse for their philosophy. Mr. Wright's architecture is an early witness of what may generally come to happen when our regional cultures absorb the lesson of the machine without losing their roots or renouncing all those elements which give landscapes and men their individualities. The formula which would exclude such a manifestation belongs as little to the future as the five orders.

Frank Lloyd Wright as Environmentalist (1966)

Reyner Banham

Reyner Banham discusses some of the environmental factors in a prairie house such as heating, lighting, and ventilating. We already learned about Wright's use of radiant heat in the Usonian house (p. 56) and are aware of his pervasive inventiveness when it came to rethinking all manner of traditional problems and needs. Wright was not, of course, always successful, at least on first try, but more often than not his ideas proved worthy and applicable and provided the client with unexpected advantages and delights.

One should add acoustics to this list of environmental factors, as anyone who has heard music or the human voice in a Wright building well knows. Another factor is visual privacy, both within and from outside the house. At the Robie house, for example, in spite of the major rooms being only a few feet from busy streets and sidewalks, the visual privacy is astonishing. When sitting in the living or dining room one's line of sight excludes the streets, cars, sidewalks, and pedestrians and begins only at the lawn across the road. Wright has inge-

Arts and Architecture 83, September 1966, pp. 26–30.
Courtesy of Reyner Banham.

niously established the floor height, the depth of the balcony,
and the height of the flower trough with such precision that—
even at night and without drapes or blinds in the windows—
those on the outside cannot see in, and those on the inside are
not forced to participate visually in the activities of the street.
Nor is this pure luck or chance because all of Wright's designs
afford a similar degree of privacy.

My interest in Wright's environmentalism began with a typically odd social evening in Chicago—a large party which assembled to sing, unrehearsed, the Bach B-minor Mass. The
venue for this distinguished and unlikely gathering was the
large living room of the Baker house in Wilmette, one of
Wright's less well-known and less well-built prairie houses;
the room a huge one-and-a-half story space with a diminutive
gallery over the fireplace. As a non-singer I was parked among
the basses at the back of the room, next to the fireplace. Suddenly it struck me that the conductor, who was standing on the
window seat in the bay window some thirty feet from the fire,
was perspiring far more freely than the *Kyrie* would seem to
justify. But, looking down at the fireplace, I saw that the fire
was not even lit.

It has been put to me that only a visitor from an underdevel-
oped country like Britain could be so naive as to suppose that
rooms are heated by fireplaces. But my naive surprise started
me on a systematic investigation of the way this, and other,
prairie houses were heated. I discovered that the main heat-
source for the Baker house living room was a large hot water
radiator, beautifully detailed into the window seat on which
our conductor has been standing. It was not an afterthought,
the carpentry of the window-seat, and of the grilles for the hot
air, is conspicuously of the same material, style and time as
the rest of the window structure, and as integral with the design as the large plant-box outside.

The complete assembly, indoors and out, can be regarded as a
single environmental device, controlling heat, light, view, ven-

tilation and (with the help of the overhang of the roof) shade as well. Not only are the parts unified as a structure, they work together as well, and this it appeared to me could be an epitome of the way the parts of the whole house worked. For instance—and it is a very crucial instance—the hot water for this radiator reaches it through pipes in the wainscot (there being no cellar) so that the living room was to some extent heated all round its three exposed sides. In the bitter Chicago winter—there were twenty inches of fresh snow in the garden on the night of the sing-party—such perimeter heating seems an eminently reasonable proposition.

But hardly an economical proposition in a room with so much exposed exterior wall made of lightweight materials, a continuous clerestory at cornice level, and a roof too skimpy to provide much thermal insulation.

My examination of the Baker house, and a knowledge of the Chicago climate, suggested a convincing-looking hypothesis about what the countervailing benefits might be: that a room with a triple exposure, and clerestory ventilation high under the roof might be more or less self-ventilating and self-cooling in the heat of high summer, to an extent that a more easily heated room buried in the mass of the house could never be without air-conditioning—which was not to exist in domestic sized installations until the Baker house was practically thirty years old. This hypothesis had the advantage of being doubly testable: by revisiting it in the height of the summer and by examining the literature to see if anything like this was among Wright's announced intentions.

On the first point, I was gratified to discover that the house is habitable throughout the year without recourse to air-conditioning, and I would like to add that it was not only comfortably habitable, but pleasurably so. Some south facing parts did begin to warm up towards the end of the afternoon on Midsummer Day, but the sun goes off them soon after, and the lightweight structure then rapidly sheds any excess heat. I also noted that, without any prompting or even inquiry from myself, the opening lights in the clerestory were, in fact, opened early in the day, so that cross-draft could prevent any accumulation of heated air under the shallow roof. Thus, I think one can safely take the Baker house bay window as an epitome of the way the whole house works—and not only the Baker house, but the Isabel Roberts house and, in varying degrees, most of the other prairie houses. What happens is that plan form, section, heating plant, windows, roof-form, all work together in varying combinations as the seasons vary to maintain a pleasant and equable climate within the house throughout the year.

The real mastery of environmental design exhibited by Wright in these houses lies in achieving conspicuously improved performance by taking thought about the rearrangement of known and familiar architectural elements. For Wright at least, environmental machinery was an aid, not a determinant, in the creation of form—as he himself makes clear in the only written statement that bears directly on his intentions in the prairie houses. This was in the introduction he wrote for the German publication of his work in 1910; in the passage that confirms my suspicions about the relationship of heating method to plan form, he manages to keep practically every other consequence and cause in view at the same time:

"Another modern opportunity is afforded by our effective system of hot water heating. By this means the forms of building may be more completely articulated, with light and air on several sides. By keeping the ceilings low, the walls may be opened with a series of windows to the outer air, the flowers and trees, the prospects, and one may live as comfortably as before, less shut in. It is also possible to spread the building which once—in our climate of extremes—was a compact box cut into compartments, into a more organic expression, making a house in the garden or in the country a delightful thing in relation to either or both."

When the Robie house was finally recognized as a building of such quality as to have some claim on the national conscience of the United States, the Historic American Buildings Survey duly recorded it in a set of measured drawings. For which we thank them, but this was a perfect example of the revolutionary nature of a building being obscured by the pre-revolutionary means employed to record it. As is customary in the traditional practice of measured drawing, the Robie house has been measured only from visible surface to visible surface—but half the quality of the house lies behind the surfaces, above the ceiling and under the floor; for this, the last of the prairie houses, was the one where Wright essayed his most radical experiments in perimeter heating, and effectively took control for the first time of electric lighting [diagrams 1, 2].

The house consists, substantially, of a long two-story block parallel with 58th Street (east-west, that is). The roof of the two-story block overhangs impressively to east and west—at the east it provides a covered entry to the kitchen wing; at the west it provides shelter against the afternoon sun.

To the south (and north too, for the sake of symmetry) the overhang is less impressive, but exactly deep enough, as I shall show later. At first floor-slab level on the south side, however, the balcony of the living room comes far enough forward to keep the ground floor fairly constantly in the shade. This is important because the ground floor and the small, almost sun-less entrance court on the north side together act as a cold-air tank to keep the whole house cool in summer. On a sweltering June afternoon, it will be appreciably chilly in the entrance hall, pleasantly temperate in the first-floor living room, and warm, but not intolerably so, in the master bedroom up under the roof—and this with every window shut.

With windows opened, however, the main living room may be ventilated in a number of ways: doors, windows may be opened at either end; the entire south front consists of glass doors giving on to the balcony, and the rear windows at the western end, overlooking the entrance court may also be opened, to exploit north-south breezes. All opening lights are protected by internal fly-screens, which are part of the original

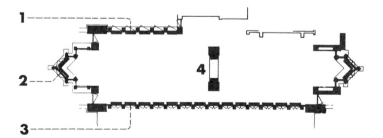

Diagram 1 F. C. Robie house, Chicago, Illinois. Plan showing heating elements and window openings. 1. Boxed radiators under rear windows 2. Hot pipes concealed behind cupboards 3. Heaters under brass grilles in floor 4. Central fireplace

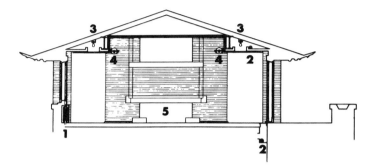

Diagram 2 F. C. Robie house, Chicago, Illinois. Section through living room. 1. Boxed radiators under windows 2. Hot water pipes 3. Concealed lights in roof-space 4. Glass lighting globes 5. Central fireplace

design. Effectively, the living room has exposure on, not three, but three-and-a-half sides, and for exactly that much of its perimeter it is heated. Under the opening windows of the north side there are dwarf radiators boxed into neat, grated enclosures; in the V-shaped ends of the room heat is supplied by hot pipes buried at the back of the built-in cupboards, slots being provided in the deep sills for the heated air to emerge; and all along the south side there are heating elements buried under the floor beneath a brass grille in front of each glass door.

The lighting arrangements patently are part of the original design. The glass globes in square japonnaiserie frames along the edge of the ceiling are familiar enough from photographs in the standard literature, but what such pictures rarely make plain enough is that the wooden slatted grilles let into the lower part of the ceiling, one to each bay like the brass grilles in the foor, have always had electric light bulbs mounted above them in the roof space. Thus, the direct luminescence in the central space of the room was supplemented by an outer band of more diffused light, dappled by the simple device of making abstract patterns with cubes of oak inserted between the slats of the grille. Electric lighting was just over twenty years old in Chicago when Fred Robie commissioned the house; Wright was one of that uniquely fortunate generation of architects who were young enough to have worked their professional careers entirely in the electrical age, but were old enough to recall the environmental miseries of the gas age that preceded it. Not all that generation profited by this good fortune as crisply as Wright did. In the year of the Robie house, Behrens can be found still designing dangling fittings with naked bulbs and elaborately ineffective fabric draped shades. Wright was one of the first architects to appreciate the creative consequences of the fact that electric lighting involves no exposed flame, generates very little heat, needs no draft of air or oxygen to keep it going and produces no noxious fumes that have to be cleared away—and for all these reasons can be enclosed or concealed in spaces and places where no lighting could safely or usefully have gone before.

But even electric lights do produce some heat and thus generate convective currents of warmed air, which raises an intriguing possibility: that the wooden grilles and electric lights may be part of a system for exploiting the roof-space (to put it no higher) as a ventilating device. If the warmed air from the lamps, or from the pipe next to the grilles, wanted to convect away anywhere, there would be room for it to escape between the flange of the structural I-beam and the underside of the roof-covering, whose slope it could follow into the central roof-space. Where would it go then? The introduction to *Wasmuth* makes a helpful suggestion again, on this topic too:

"The gently sloping roofs grateful to the prairie do not leave large air-spaces above the rooms, and so the chimney has grown in dimensions and importance and in hot weather ventilates the circulating air-spaces beneath the roofs, fresh air entering beneath the eaves through openings easily closed in winter."

The Robie house certainly exemplifies these propositions: a square grille is let into the soffit of the long overhang at each end of the main roof, and the chimney has an added limb on its western side, clearly exhibiting the pattern of missing bricks which signals a ventilator in Wright's work of this period—it shows up in both the Larkin building and the Isabel Roberts house. Warm air spillage over the recessed lights could well have contributed to this ventilating process, even when the grilles under the eaves were closed in winter.

But the most intriguing question of this sort raised by the Robie house concerns, not the newest source of environmental power, but the oldest—sunlight. I have already mentioned the seemingly inadequate overhang of the southern eaves of the house, but it only seems inadequate because we forget how far south Chicago is: the same latitude as Istanbul or Rome. The sun stands high in summer, so high that at noon on Midsummer's Day the shadow of the eaves just kisses the woodwork at the bottom of the glass doors, leaving the glass in shadow and thus unheated. Give or take a quarter of an inch, it hits that woodwork line so exactly, so neatly, that it takes your breath away. It is difficult to believe that it is not deliberate, but equally difficult to believe that if Mr. Wright had done it on purpose he would not have drawn attention to the fact somewhere in print.

Unlike most previous (and too many subsequent) employments of environmental aids, they have not here been clipped on to a conventionally conceived structure to ameliorate its inadequate performance. In the prairie houses the structure, its solids, voids and overhangs, and the mechanics whether they consume coal, gas, kerosene or electricity, work together in a manner that deserves the favorite Wrightian epithet of "organic"—and were conceived as working together in this way from the start. Nothing is merely an amelioration or corrective of something else; hardly any single function is performed by any one element alone, most are the working result of elements functioning together with the practiced ingenuity and concealed craft normally found in vernaculars that have been a thousand years in the growing.

The Anatomy of Wright's Aesthetic (1968)

Richard C. MacCormac

In An Autobiography *and elsewhere Wright praises the posi-tive aspects of his Froebel kindergarten education, to which he attributes much that governed his own method of design. He was introduced to the system at the age of nine, after his mother learned of it while visiting the Centennial Exposition of 1876. The Froebel "gifts," as they are called, consist of geo-metric blocks and colored cardboard shapes with which the child makes patterns and constructions upon a squared unit grid. The first "gift" consists of a single cube, sphere, and cyl-inder and only when the potential of this gift is completely mastered is an additional gift meted out. The emphasis is upon pure geometric forms and the abstract, symmetrical pat-terns they produce upon the grid. Grant C. Manson has shown (*"Wright in the Nursery," Architectural Review, *June 1953) that approximate models of the Larkin Building, Unity Temple, and other Wright buildings can be constructed with these blocks. Richard C. MacCormac carries the analysis beyond a purely formal comparison in order to elucidate the basic method of unit design that these gifts instilled in Wright.*

Architectural Review 143, February 1968, pp. 143–146.
Reprinted by permission, *Architectural Review*, London.

While MacCormac speaks of tartan-like patterns, this does not negate the fact that there is an underlying, uniform grid. The tartan effect results from the fact that certain lines in the grid, due to Wright's alignment of major and minor elements in the design, receive more emphasis than others. The tartans of MacCormac can be converted into regular grids by reintroducing these less emphasized, and therefore deleted, lines—a clarification that MacCormac agrees should have been mentioned in his original text.

Wright wrote that "All the buildings I have ever built, large and small, are fabricated upon a unit system—as the pile of a rug is stitched into the warp. Thus each structure is an ordered fabric. Rhythm, consistent scale of parts, and economy of construction are greatly facilitated by this simple expedient—a mechanical one absorbed in a final result to which it has given more consistent texture, a more tenuous quality as a whole." (Wendingen, *1925, p. 57.)*

Frank Lloyd Wright's acknowledgement of his kindergarten experience and the outward resemblance between his buildings and the illustrations of the "gifts" in the Froebel manual are already well known. Though remarkable, these comparisons do little more than indicate the source of Wright's characteristic "style." Closer investigation—at the level of intention and organization rather than simply of appearance—suggests that the kindergarten was of a much more radical significance for Wright, that it provided him with a philosophy and with a design discipline to realize his architecture.

Froebel did not intend his patterns merely to have aesthetic appeal. He conceived them as the instrument of a system of education based upon a pantheistic conception of nature. The aim of this was two-fold, intellectual and spiritual; an understanding of natural law would simultaneously develop the powers of reason and convey a sense of the harmony and order of God: "God's works reflect the logic of his spirit and human education cannot do anything better than imitate the logic of nature."

Such a discipline must have made a deep impression upon Wright. It presented him with a comprehensive vision in which aesthetics were inseparable from universal principles of form. In the light of such an inheritance we may appreciate his extraordinary confidence in the absolute validity of his architecture as an expression of natural law and his almost messianic belief in his role as an architect. The extent to which he was indeed affected becomes apparent if one compares extracts from the text of the manual and examples from the exercises with some of his own characteristic statements.

"The child is first taught to take the cube out of the box undivided in order to inculcate alike the sense of order and the idea of completeness. . . . In life we find no isolation. One part of the cube, therefore, must never be left apart from or without relation to the whole. The child will thus become accustomed to treating all things in life as bearing a certain relation to one another."

"Any building should be complete," said Wright, "including all within itself. Instead of many things one thing. . . . Perfect correlation, integration is life. It is the first principle of any growth that the thing grown be no mere aggregation . . . and integration means that no part of anything is of any great value except as it be integrate part of the harmonious whole."

In each of the Froebel patterns the parts have to some extent surrendered their identity to the whole to which they contribute [diagram 1]. For Wright this was a basic recognition; parts added, porches, verandahs and balconies, should not be sensed as additional but should seem intrinsic, as extensions of inner structure. To help the child arrange the blocks, the kindergartener could provide a table-top ruled with a grid. The

Writings on Wright

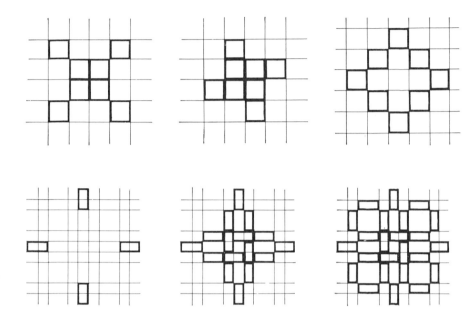

Diagram 1 (Top) In the Froebel patterns the parts have . . . surrendered their identity to the whole.

Diagram 2 (Bottom) A typical pattern consists of two interpenetrating cruciforms breaking through a square.

discipline of a grid, combined with modular components, engenders the kind of correlation described. Wright appreciated this in his own planning. "What we call standardization is seen to be fundamental groundwork in architecture. All things in nature exhibit this tendency to crystallize. . . . The kindergarten training, as I have shown, proved an unforeseen asset . . . a properly proportional unit system kept all to scale like a tapestry, a consistent fabric of interdependent related units, however various."

Given these disciplines, T-square and set-square were the obvious tools of Wright's aesthetic. It is characteristic of his sketch-plans that they are matted with exploratory lines—a mesh refined and tightened to correlate appropriate parts. "This principle of design was natural, inevitable for me. It is based on the straight line technique of T-square and triangle. It was inherent in the Froebel system of kindergarten training given to me by my mother."

Some of the exercises are composed with rectangular blocks rather than cubes, and these set up a tartan, rather than an even, modular grid. A typical pattern [diagram 2] consists of two interpenetrating cruciforms breaking through a square, establishing an interdependence of interior structure and external shape comparable to that in Wright's work. In fact it is surprising to find Froebel anticipating one of Wright's most fundamental propositions; for the handbook claims that the gifts "enable the child to strive after the comprehension of both external appearances and inner conditions" and emphasizes that the outward shape of the patterns is conditioned by the geometry of the whole. Similarly, the exterior forms of Wright's buildings usually project internal spaces, the precedent of the Froebel exercises suggesting that he started from a geometric premise rather than from some personal spatial insight: "This sense of the within, or of the room itself, or of the rooms themselves, I now saw as the great thing to be expressed as architecture. This sense of interior space, made exterior as architecture, transcended all that had gone before. . . . Hitherto all classical or ancient buildings had been great masses or blocks of building material sculpted into shape outside and hollowed out to live in."

Comparisons of this kind, between flat patterns and architecture, must take into consideration the perceptual difference between seeing the whole pattern from above and grasping the overall form of a building from its perimeter. Wright understood this problem when he wrote, "I have endeavoured to establish a harmonious relationship between ground plan and elevation of these buildings, considering the one as a solution and the other as an expression. . . ." This is aptly illustrated by one of the models in the manual, which is an alternative to the flat patterns. The rather unbelievable "bath" [diagram 3] translates the characteristic intersection of square and cruciform into three dimensions. The overall structure is conveyed by the elevational distinction between the two figures, the interplay of steps and podium at each end depend upon a similar expression.

The approach to Wright's prairie houses, which follows, has been developed from the preceding analyses. The evolution of typical features of the period, the overhanging roofs, the podia and the projecting cubic forms, is considered as an extension of the kindergarten system rather than simply the invention of a personal idiom. Wright's architecture, often supposed the most impervious to formal analysis, reveals a surprising geometric rigour. The plan [diagram 4] of the George Blossom house of 1892 is, for example, obviously analogous to the intersecting squares and cruciforms of the patterns. Elevationally the plan is conveyed by the recessed central bays, which suggest that the entrance porch and balcony are extensions of the plan rather than additions. In comparison, the front and side elevations of the Winslow house of the following year are far less explicit. The exterior of the Husser house [of 1899, diagram 5] is in this respect the antithesis of the front elevations of the Winslow house. No longer conceived as a separate entity wrapped around the plan, it is the product of the various components which make up the interlocking volumes of the interior; this is the crux of the idea which Wright's architecture inherited from the kindergarten.

It will be seen that the Husser house is developed from an underlying grid. From the plan of the Charles S. Ross house of 1902 it is possible to abstract a perfect tartan [diagram 6] and from this the volumes of the building can be projected exactly, in the same way as in the case of the Froebel bath. The pre-

More Recent Evaluation

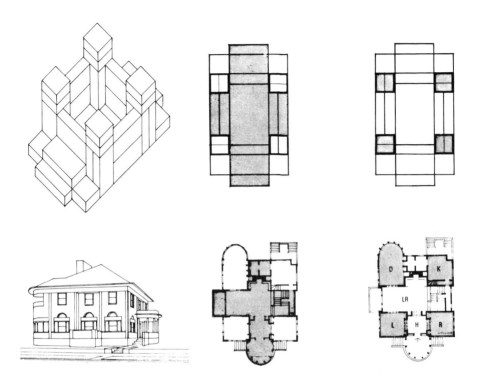

Diagram 3 (Top) The characteristic intersection of square and cruciform into three dimensions.

Diagram 4 (Bottom) The plan of the George Blossom house (1892) is
. . . analogous to the intersecting squares and cruciforms of the patterns.

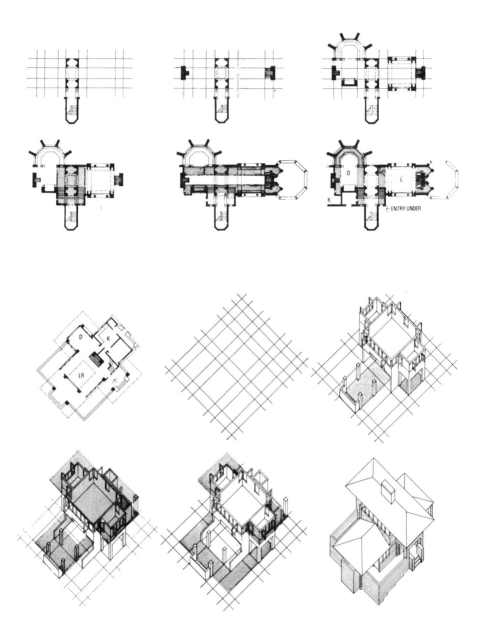

Diagram 5 (Top) The exterior of the Husser house . . . is no longer conceived as a separate entity wrapped around the plan.

Diagram 6 (Bottom) From the plan of the Charles S. Ross house of 1902 it is possible to abstract a perfect tartan.'

dominant figure is a cruciform with another contained within it, comparable with the Froebel cruciforms on a tartan grid [diagram 2]. This kind of figure was to be the basis of most of Wright's later houses. In this example, the inner cruciform is expressed with porches and balconies and the outer with the roofs, which are extended geometrically from the main cube of the house. The raised portion of the living-room ceiling and bedroom casements also correspond with the inner grid. The podium further develops the theme of modules contained one within another by expressing a yet wider module, which is related to the volume it surrounds as the eaves are to the volumes beneath them. The same grid underlies the little Barton house of the following year [diagram 7], distinguished by a more consistent structural discipline which perhaps reflects Wright's preoccupation with the large-scale structure of the Larkin Building at this time. The plan is again composed of crosses, one within another, the exterior walls and main piers of the porch representing the outer figure, and the bay-window of the kitchen, the living-room flower boxes and the extended veranda of the porch representing the inner one. Other components submit as rigidly to the pattern; the living-room windows, with their large flat sills, and the chimney and dining-room sideboard expose the wider module of the tartan, the lesser module being taken up by the structure throughout. The grid also relates the house to the adjacent Martin house, with which it forms a larger group.

The detached corner piers of the Robert Evans house of 1908, [diagram 8] have the same effect. To use an analogy with the kindergarten—it is almost as if they defined the extent of the ruled table-top within which the pattern stands. Wright's progress can be measured by comparing the Evans house with the Blossom house [diagram 4] based upon the same cross-in-square plan sixteen years before. The windows of the Blossom house conform to an elevational discipline unrelated to the interior. Those of the Evans house express the cruciform component projecting between the blank corner units which establish the square. The tentative projections of the Blossom house have become, in the Evans house, the cantilevered roofs of veranda and porte cochere. Beneath these the inner modules of the grid are represented by components of various heights, flower boxes, balustrades and bay windows arranged

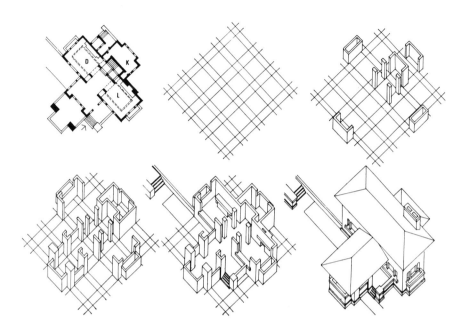

Diagram 7 The same grid underlies the little Barton house of the following year.

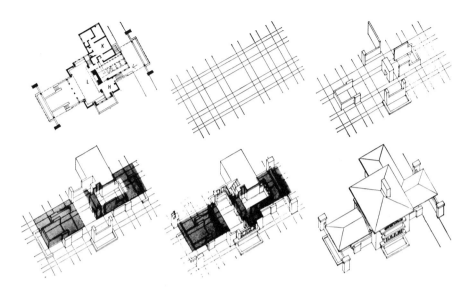

Diagram 8 The detached corner piers of the Robert Evans house of 1908 . . . suggest that the main volume of the building 'stands' within the grid rather than around it.

so that they overlap but do not obscure one another. With this assembly of parts, characteristic of the mature prairie period, Wright translated the patterns of the kindergarten into a three-dimensional system of architecture.

Wright and the Destruction of the Box (1979)

H. Allen Brooks

It is common these days for writers to extol the virtues of Wrightian space, yet one notices how consistently these same writers avoid any attempt to define it, and how they make no distinction between Wright's type of space and the interiors of other twentieth-century architects such as Le Corbusier. In short, it seems evident that they fail to comprehend how Wright created it. A similar situation exists among practicing architects who profess indebtedness to Wright's ideas on space because if one asks them how Wright constructed it, they usually lack an explanation.

A book such as this would be incomplete without some discussion of this basic topic, which should be at the core of all Wright studies. But, incredible as it seems, nothing excepting Wright's own remarks has yet been written on this theme. Therefore I have prepared the following text.

Frank Lloyd Wright wrote eloquently and often about the destruction of the box, and writers ever since have indiscriminately used such phrases as "open space" and "flowing space," whether they are discussing interiors by Wright, Le

Journal of the Society of Architectural Historians 38, March 1979, pp. 7–14.
© Copyright 1979, Society of Architectural Historians.

Corbusier, or any number of twentieth-century architects. In so doing they reveal basic misconceptions concerning Wright's achievement: Wright's spaces are more open and flowing than those that existed previously, but they are also profoundly different both in their design and in their psychological impact from the interiors with which they are often associated.

When Wright entered the profession late in the 1880s the Shingle Style, or Queen Anne, had largely spent its force. From these styles he inherited the idea of using generous openings between principal rooms and of occasionally basing his layout upon an axial or cruciform plan. Until about 1900 this exerted a considerable influence on his work.

But Shingle Style planning did not call into question the basic concept of the room. The four walls, joined at the corners, and the uniform floor and ceiling remained; the room continued to be a box. What had changed was the degree of openness between the rooms and this was achieved by increasing the size of the door (the hinged door gave way to a sliding door, or might be eliminated altogether) until it approached the size of the wall itself. The specific organization and use of the room was not affected. What one gained was a sense of spaciousness while looking from room to room. What one lost was a sense of privacy.

Wright realized this. He also saw that room specialization exceeded realistic limits with each social or family function requiring a separate room. One box, neatly labeled, was placed beside another and a series of these boxes made up the home. This was nothing new; the room as a box had existed since earliest times. Yet Wright soon redefined the concept of interior space, and he began this process by dismembering the traditional box.

The Ross house (1902) at Delavan Lake will ideally serve to demonstrate how he approached the problem. Being among the earliest of Wright's prairie houses, changes in it can be noted at a rudimentary stage in their development, and being a small house, it is not so difficult to analyze as the more complex Willits or Martin houses of about the same date. And because the plan derives from a Shingle Style house, it is easy to compare and contrast differences.

From Bruce Price's Kent house (1885) at Tuxedo Park Wright accepted, in designing the Ross house, the basic layout of the plan. Both are cruciform in shape, both have the same disposition of similar rooms, and both have a characteristic U-shaped veranda around the front [diagrams 1 and 2]. Different, but essential, is the subtle spatial relation in Wright's design between the dining and the living rooms.

Wright attacked the traditional room at its point of greatest strength—at the corner. He dissolved the corner between the dining and living rooms at the Ross house by permitting one room to penetrate into the other. If the living room walls are visually extended to their point of contact, the corner is at the dining room table. A similar extension of the dining room walls makes a corner located well within the living room. At a primary level, therefore, both rooms are making use of an area within the other room's space; this is totally different from Shingle Style space [diagram 3]. The area of overlap also serves as connector (the corridor or doorway) between the rooms. Thus Wright obtains several uses from this single space and he can reduce the size and cost of the house accordingly—without making the house seem any smaller.

This, when demonstrated, is a simple idea (most great ideas are simple ones) yet in its ultimate implications it is one of the most important "discoveries" ever made in architecture.

In Wright's work, space loses its fixed value and acquires a relative one. In that it depends upon experience and observation it is empirical space, contingent upon the viewer rather than possessing an independent reality of its own. It relates to individuals and their changing position within that space.

It should be noted that visual space in the Ross house extends well beyond the point of overlap between two rooms. Unlike the vista in a Shingle Style house, it is diagonal, not face-to-face. As a result, Wright gains more privacy and variety. The view into the neighboring room is restricted, and changes markedly as one moves from place to place [diagram 3, right].

Outside corners were more difficult for Wright to eliminate than interior ones, yet once he got rid of them his "invisible corners" (of mitered glass) became one of the hallmarks of the modern movement. In the Ross house he took a major first

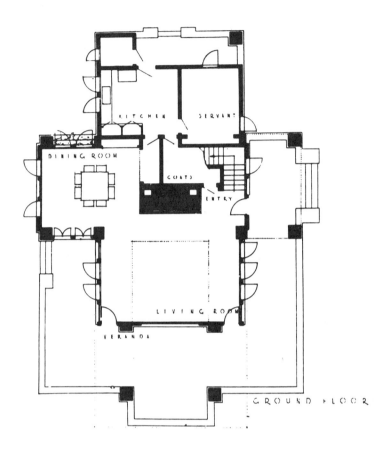

Diagram 1 Frank Lloyd Wright, Charles S. Ross house, Delevan Lake, Wisconsin, 1902. Plan. (Hitchcock, *In the Nature of Materials*)

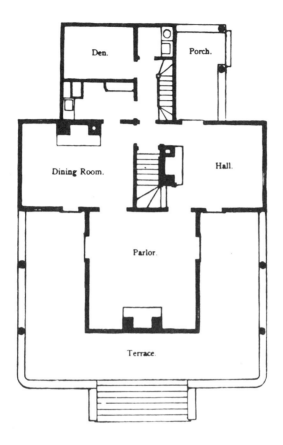

Diagram 2 Bruce Price, William Kent house, Tuxedo Park, New York, 1885. Plan. (Sheldon, *Artistic Country-Seats*, 1886–1887)

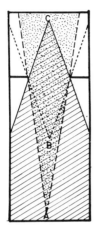 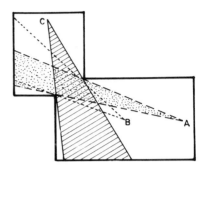

Diagram 3 Shingle Style vs. Frank Lloyd Wright. Left: typical Shingle Style plan with large openings between the principal rooms. Right: in a Wright house one room penetrates into the other at the corners.

A, B, and C show the angle of vision, taken from identical positions, into the neighboring room. Wright achieves more privacy and variety.

Room dimensions in these two plans are identical.

step in this direction. The glazed doors leading to the veranda are set flush against the corner, visually eliminating the right angle at this point. As one looks down the length of the lateral walls one's sight is not stopped at the corner but passes outside through the doors. At the other end, the left hand wall has no visible inside corner where it dissolves into the dining room. It is beginning to assume the character of a freestanding slab. When Wright completely freed the wall from its corners, it did become a slab, and once it became a slab he was free to move it around or divide it up at will. When this happened, the room as a box was destroyed.

Yet boxes have tops and bottoms as well as sides, and already at the Ross house Wright began manipulating the height of the ceiling in order to enhance the activities taking place underneath. The dotted line on the plan indicates a higher ceiling in the front-center of the living room—the area where one normally stands. Near the fireplace, along the windows of the outside walls, and in the dining room—all places where one normally sits—the ceiling height is lower.

The axonometric sketch [diagram 4] clarifies what has been said. To the left is what Wright set out to destroy, a house made up of a series of boxes, each placed beside or above the other, and each with its single specialized use. Enlarging the openings between contiguous boxes (as in the Shingle Style) created a sense of greater openness, but if carried too far, the smaller rooms would merge and become a single larger room with one relinquishing its identity to the other (a process that again produces a series of boxes).

The axonometric at the right indicates Wright's first step in destroying the box. He interlocks two rooms so that part of each space is given over to the other. The corners (the least useful part of the room) are destroyed and a controlled view into the adjacent area is opened up. This view, which is diagonal and pinched at the point of interlock, is limited and leaves much of the adjoining area obscure, introducing a sense of mystery into the spatial sequence. Mystery is an essential element in Wrightian space; he never resolves all visual questions at once; rather he holds in reserve something to be examined later. To assist in this process of limiting and controlling the view and guarding the privacy of the adjoining spaces, Wright

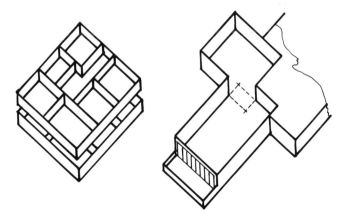

Diagram 4 Left: typical house composed of box-like rooms. Right: Wright's first step in destroying the box. Rooms are interlocked, usually at the corners, with each relinquishing part of its space to the other. Sometimes this occurs at different levels creating balconies, split-levels, and varying floor and ceiling heights. The corner has been dissolved.

screens openings by various means—for example, vertical wooden slats combined with low bookshelves (Willits house), walls that do not reach the ceiling (Roberts and Hanna houses), fireplaces or chimneys that open into the neighboring space (Martin and Robie houses).

The axonometric also indicates how spaces of different height can interpenetrate, the one imparting to the other its ceiling and/or floor height. In its simplest form, this creates a balcony (Roberts, Baker, Millard at Pasadena) or "split-level" type of house (Davidson, Pope, Grant). In the sophisticated arrangement preferred by Wright it produced two or more ceiling heights that overlapped and interpenetrated throughout the house (and on the exterior as well), the height being carefully related to the human activity underneath. Wright perfected this in his Usonian houses, yet he had mastered the idea prior to 1910.

Before continuing, two points will be developed further in order to clarify and amplify what already has been said. First, a consistency of design permeates every aspect of Wright's work, imparting to it a unity that is total and complete. Consequently, the concept behind the destruction of the box found expression in a wide variety of things designed by Wright. Note, for example, the interior pier at Unity Temple [figure 10]. The wood stripping (Wright's word for trim) is not used in the traditional manner in order to define a two-dimensional rectangle on the surface, with a separate rectangle for each face of the pier, but instead the stripping passes around the corner to unite the two surfaces into a single *three-dimensional* form. This destroys the age-old concept of the corner just as effectively as Wright destroyed it in the region between the living and dining rooms at the Ross house. This three-dimensional manner of thinking, which is characteristic of Wright's work, can also be seen in the way he often unites ceilings and walls by this simple device, as in the Robie house [figure 12]. Spatially Wright dissolves the corner and makes it transparent; the next logical step was to use mitered glass instead of opaque materials, a system Wright perfected early in the twenties.

The second point concerns the center of the wall. Unlike the architects of the Shingle Style or their twentieth-century coun-

terparts, Wright did not create large openings in the wall (unless when uniting interior and exterior space) since this would
lead to a loss of interior privacy. Instead, if he wished to relate
two rooms face-to-face, he substituted for the wall a screen
that could be walked around or looked over. The Robie house
is a perfect example of this. The dining room and living room
have their outer walls in common, but the "wall" that sepa-
rates the two rooms is a freestanding fireplace [figure 12]. The
flues go up the sides making possible a large opening in the
chimney mass at the level of the ceiling. From either room one
can look back to the adjoining ceiling, and this adds a sense of
spaciousness without diminishing privacy. Similarly—and this
is of great importance—one has an unbroken view along the
lateral walls of these two connected rooms. Due to the absence of corners (no visual "stop" signs) it is impossible to tell
where these outer walls terminate, or when they are no longer
part of the space in which you are standing. This is especially
effective on the street side of the Robie house: the uninter-
rupted range of French doors is simultaneously part of both
rooms. No visual break, outside or inside, denotes the limits of
either space. This is so, as already explained, because Wrightian space depends on the position of the viewer and not on a
predetermined boundary.

By visually extending space, Wright achieved a sense of ex-
pansiveness that the actual dimensions of the building would
seem to deny. This was immensely important for Wright's
later work; it holds great potential for the future of architecture, yet even in his smallest prairie houses Wright utilized this
means with stunning effect (for example his 1906 project,
"Fireproof House for $5,000," in *Ladies Home Journal*, 1907).

The implications of freeing the wall from its terminals were
immense, and further consequences of this fact were soon realized by Wright. Once the wall was freed from its corners it
became a slab, and once it became a slab, it was no longer
locked into a fixed position in space; it could be rotated on its
axis, it could be divided into smaller slabs, it could (as later
occurred in Cubist painting) be reassembled and reintegrated
to define something new. The evolution of this process is illustrated in diagram 5 where the first sketch-plan, A, represents a
typical rectangular room with its four walls locked together at
the corners. In the second diagram, B, the corners are elimi-

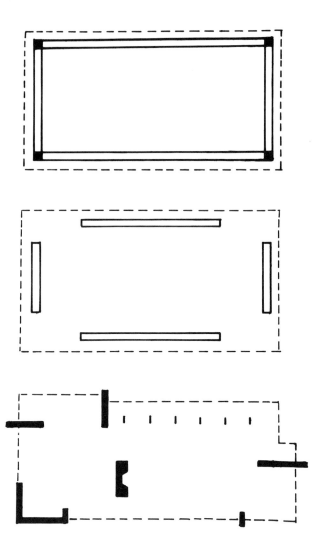

Diagram 5 A: typical room with walls joined at four corners. B: Wright's first step—eliminate the corners, thus turning the walls into freestanding, movable slabs. C: Wright's second step—define, by reassembling segments of these slabs, a new spatial context that integrates the former functions of the demolished rooms; this is a schematic plan of a Usonian house (author after Wright).

nated and the corner posts removed. The walls have become independent planes or slabs, each clearly separate from one another. Taken together they define (rather than precisely enclose) an area that is similar to the first diagram, except for the region near the corners. This sketch is analogous to the Ross house plan already discussed.

An intermediary stage between B and C is exemplified in the plan of the Martin house [1904, figure 4], which was published in the 1910 Wasmuth portfolio and therefore widely available in Europe (cf. Mies van der Rohe's 1923 project for a brick country house, and the work of the de Stijl group, for instance.) The striking fact about this plan is the absence of walls in the traditional sense. Only piers and slabs are used, set in a charged, yet dynamically balanced, paired relation one with the other. A screen of windows, as protection against the weather, connects these points of support, which define the limits of the house and the various spaces therein.

The third diagram, C, illustrates what Wright achieved once the wall was free of its terminals. Here even the formality and axial symmetry of the Martin plan (which owed much to Beaux-Arts planning) are gone and instead there is an abstract pattern of reassembled parts. This pattern represents the schematic plan of one of Wright's Usonian houses in which the living space contains many "rooms." Integrated into this new spatial environment can be a living room, a dining room, a hallway, a den, and perhaps other rooms as well. They are defined within the context of the larger space. Thus one or two spur walls, a lower ceiling, a different fenestration create the setting for a dining room, other combinations are used to establish a den, and so on. These are sometimes difficult to identify in plan, but when one experiences the three-dimensional space the function of each area is absolutely clear—and this is independent of the furniture grouping. Each use-space utilizes and participates in part of the adjoining spaces (and they in it) just as we saw in a more rudimentary form at the Ross house. Only bedrooms and baths retain their integrity as private rooms.

Our attention thus far has focused upon the walls of rooms rather than on floors and ceilings. Yet these were also essential to Wright's manipulation of space and they gained in importance as the actual size of the house decreased and more and more "rooms" were integrated into the basic living space. Either two or three ceiling heights were used in his smallest houses and, if the character of the landscape permitted, he would raise or lower the floor as well.

With a change in ceiling height Wright could psychologically define the boundaries of a use-area in a region where the walls had been removed. Thus the outer limits of a low ceiling might "stake out" a dining room, the ceiling height harmonizing with the seated activity of dining. All areas primarily designed for sitting and for intimate thoughts and conversation had lower ceilings than those designated for standing or walking or working. The miracle is that Wright did not end up with an overhead mess of conflicting ceiling heights but instead succeeded in creating something that was as unobtrusive and restful as it was effective.

Floors present a special problem but occasionally Wright introduced a single change in level, as in the Willits and Davidson houses dating from the prairie period. Later, for instance at the Palmer house, he might employ an upward step to dissuade the visitor from approaching the bedroom wing, or, as at the Pope house, to increase the sense of nobility and spaciousness as one descends from the entrance into the more public regions of the house [figure 25].

The dimensions and placement of these various space-defining elements (such as screens, slabs, piers, ceilings, fireplaces) was never haphazard or arbitrary but was always controlled and governed by what Wright called a "unit system." He made no secret of this system which developed, he said, from his Froebel kindergarten training. Occasionally he even published the units under illustrations of his buildings [figure 4]. Yet he never explicitly explained how the system worked. We had to await Robert MacCormac's published research before having a plausible explanation; his analytic drawing of the Ross house indicates the grid of units that controlled the size and placement of each element in the plan [diagram 6, p. 170]. Later Wright applied this system to elevations as well.

More Recent Evaluation

An essential aspect of Wright's organic architecture is the idea that interior space must find exterior expression. That this occurred is revealed by even the most cursory review of his buildings. In the closed, stately forms of the Winslow façade (1893) space is imprisoned and there is no sense of outward release. With the prairie houses the wall quickly loses its role a container of space as increasingly it is shattered into piers and screens; horizontal elements are left visually unsupported at their terminals and become cantilevered roofs and balconies that in no way impede the outward-inward interaction of space. A comparison of the Willits (1902) and the Robie (1908) houses makes this development absolutely clear. In the years that followed, the change was one of degree, not of kind. The buildings became more informal, open, and immediate in their association with the natural surroundings. The modest-sized Usonian house was the perfect expression of this. Yet outwardly, the spatial facts of the interior could always be read. A closed, U-shaped masonry wall, lit internally only by a clearstory window under a low slab roof, was a den, a place of retreat; a higher roof and banks of glazed French doors signaled a more public living space; modest windows facing a protected court were those of a bedroom. The manifestations of the space were always apparent; they were defined, and the definition was there for all to read.

In sum, we have seen how Wright dealt with the age-old question of interior space. For him the process of its reorganization was no fanciful or playful matter, but an arduous intellectual feat. The traditional concept of the room, formed by walls joined at the corners, had existed—unchallenged—since the earliest habitations, and by the nineteenth century its proliferation (nowhere carried to a more ridiculous extreme than in the English country house) had reached, both socially and economically, illogical bounds. He recognized this and was determined to correct it. He analyzed the components of a room, which basically was a box. He realized that the corners were the most expressive element, so he demolished them first. He then dismembered intermediary walls, ceilings, and even floors. Finally, as was later to occur in synthetic Cubism, he reassembled the shattered pieces (images) in a different spatial context. He defined, rather than enclosed, the functions that rooms had served. And in accordance with his profound understanding of the human psyche, he created a physically smaller, yet psychologically more healthy, environment in which to live. This is the measure of his genius, and toward this end the destruction of the box was the first essential step.

The Domestic Architecture of Frank Lloyd Wright (1963)

Norris Kelly Smith

Norris Kelly Smith celebrates Wright's concern for both the institution of the family and the social order, this in opposition to the widely held belief that architecture is, and should be, primarily an expression of the technological potential of our age. These and other themes he later developed more fully in his book Frank Lloyd Wright: A Study in Architectural Content *(1966).*

I should like to submit that Wright's distinction as a domestic architect stemmed not so much from his inventive originality as a designer, or from his use of space or materials or structures, as from his profoundly ethical concern for the institutions of the state, the city, and the family, and for the relation of the free man to those institutions. I would celebrate, therefore, not so much Wright's modernity as what he himself recognized from the very beginning to be his conservatism.

Wright understood, as most modern architects apparently have not, that the great buildings of our past have served as structural metaphors, declaring in their own ordering something about the power of institutions to give order; affirming in their structural patterns something about those patterns of relatedness among men which make possible the existence of that more or less precarious fabric of institutionalized relationships which constitutes the state. As early as 1900, Wright

Columbia University, *Four Great Makers of Modern Architecture*, New York: Trustees of Columbia University, 1963, pp. 76–83.
Reprinted by permission, School of Architecture, Columbia University, and Norris Kelly Smith.

wrote that civilization must take the natural man to fit him for his place in this great piece of architecture we call the social state. Later, in his *Autobiography*, he declared that "since all form is a matter of structure it is a matter of government as well as a matter of architecture; a matter of the framework of a society." It was this relationship between buildings and institutions, as Wright saw it, which had made architecture the very embodiment of the "spirit of law and order."

During the nineteenth century, however, architecture had come to be put to a novel and quite different use: namely, that of conjuring up, in the single observer, emotionally charged associations with one or another of the great ages of the historical world-drama—Roman, Gothic, Renaissance, and so on. It was presumed that each of those ages had possessed a unique spirit or rhythm or tonality of its own; that the architect's function had always been to express the spirit of his age in visible forms; and, furthermore, that a great building in a given style could somehow arouse or inculcate a corresponding spiritual attitude in a modern individual—whence the enthusiasm for building Gothic churches in the days of Ruskin and Carlyle. In all this, the structure-giving role of the institution was made secondary to, or eliminated in favor of, the emotional experience of the private person.

It seems generally to be taken for granted today that the distinctively modern architecture of the twentieth century had its origins in a drastic reaction against this historicistic aberration. I would argue, on the contrary, that our mechanistic contemporary style is based on precisely those Victorian presuppositions about architecture which undergirded the Gothic revival a century ago: it results, that is, from a self-conscious attempt on the part of the architect to invent a style that will express what he presumes to be the scientific and technological spirit of our age and that will at the same time propagate and inculcate that spirit in a recalcitrant populace that inclines all too readily toward a thoroughly nonscientific emotionality, irrationality, and even violence. His concern for institutional metaphor, however, is no greater than was his eclectic predecessor's.

Taking the broadest view of the matter, then, I would celebrate Wright's memory because he brought back to life a conception of architecture as an art of eloquent affirmation concerning those institutions upon which rest the integrity and stability of the social order. The cause, as he himself avowed, was conservative, but has not architecture always been devoted to the maintenance of tradition and to the preservation of the establishment?

The greatness of Wright's architecture is bound up with his profoundly conservative commitment to an institution and to a tradition. The institution, of course, was the middle-class private family. From first to last he was a domestic architect, the greatest house-builder of his century—and for the very reason that his own relationship to the institution of the family was so charged with emotion and so ambivalent. By his earliest childhood experiences he was made aware of the trying aspects of marriage, as well as to the blessings of family solidarity, while his own much-publicized difficulties with the institution of matrimony are common knowledge. It was the strength of his architectural imagination that he found the essence of the problem of human relatedness to reside in the structure of the private family. At the very end of his life he could still write, "The true center (the only centralization allowable) in Usonian democracy is the individual in his Usonian family home. In that we have the nuclear building we will learn how to build." His concern scarcely extended beyond its limits. He was relatively indifferent to both the constitutional theory and the political realities of the United States government; and while he loved Chicago, his interest in the structure and planning of cities, as they presently exist, was confined to the residential suburb.

The tradition Wright defended was that of romanticism—specifically, that strain of romanticism that descends from Rousseau by way of Goethe, Carlyle, Emerson, Thoreau, and Whitman. Now one of the distinctive characteristics of romantic thought is its attraction toward opposite and extreme positions—in contrast to the classicist's preoccupation with the median and the norm. Wright's life and outlook were filled with apparently irreconcilable contrasts. In his very nature he was a radical and rebellious conservative, an ostentatious defender of unpretentious simplicity, a champion of machine-age modernity whose highest admiration was reserved for the culture of feudal Japan. He could advocate, in Broadacres, a program of decentralization so thoroughgoing as to eradicate the city from the landscape; but at the same time he could design the Mile-High building, which would have brought about the greatest concentration of humanity ever envisioned in the history of architecture. He was an anarchist, intransigent in his opposition to the claims of governmental authority, and simultaneously a pan-archist, capable of conceiving a society in which virtually every aspect of life would be brought under the supervision of the state. All this is part and parcel of a tradition which can be traced back at least as far as Rousseau, between whose books, *Emile* and *The Social Contract*, one finds this kind of polar opposition to exist; and beyond Rousseau there lies a venerable religious tradition in which paradise is envisioned at one and the same time as an open garden and as a fortress city.

The ethical tradition is a very old one. However, the art of architecture has generally done service in defense of its collective and institutional aspect rather than, and even at the expense of, its personal and individualizing one. The art of building has all too often been the monopoly of a ruling aristocracy, serving the special interests of that class. Today it is no longer the instrument of that class; institutions claim less for themselves, individuals claim more. Yet it does not follow that the values of personal freedom are all-sufficient—that the values of loyalty and commitment need no longer be matters of concern to us—that we have no desire to experience a meaningful and responsible participation in the body politic, no anxiety about the possibility of doing so. Not at all. There is much in modern life that diminishes the ethical stature of man—much that suggests it is possibly the case that when the traditions and institutions of our society become meaningless, our personal freedom becomes meaningless, also. Such was Wright's conviction, at least, and he was concerned throughout his life to defend and to reinterpret that polaristic tradition of high spiritual tension to which Bellini and Rousseau and Whitman, in their different ways, had been devoted, and to reassess the institution of the family in the light of that tradition.

Let me conclude with a quotation from the late Albert Camus. "As a result of rejecting everything, even the traditions of his art, the contemporary artist gets the illusion that he is creating his own rule and eventually takes himself for God. At the same time he thinks he can create his reality himself. But cut off from his society, he will create nothing but formal or abstract works, thrilling as experiences but devoid of the fecundity we associate with true art, which is called upon to unite." While many an architect today would readily acknowledge the applicability of Camus' criticism to recent painting, there appears to be a strong inclination in the profession to believe, as I have already suggested, that the modern architect is doing what architects have always done—that is, to meet his society's needs by exploiting its technological potentialities, and in so doing to express the spirit or character of his age. But all of that has nothing to do with the ethical and spiritual traditions of our society, nor with the traditional concern of the architect to interpret, through structural metaphors, the patterns of relatedness that make it possible for a society to endure. Wright's architecture, I believe, possessed the fecundity of true art precisely for the reason that he was not cut off from such traditions but recognized, instead, that what the artists of all ages have been called upon to do is to reassess, in the light of a changing situation, that body of meaning and of civilizing truth which has been received. And in an age that values originality and inventiveness, he demonstrated that that can be done without adopting the architectural vocabulary of an earlier period.

I do not mean to say that Wright's buildings should serve as models for a new generation of architects, or that the traditions of Rousseauistic romanticism are preeminently worthy of our regard. My contention is only that great architecture arises, not out of technological achievement, but out of a warm and sympathetic commitment to the institutions and the traditions of a civilization.

An Architect in Search of Democracy: Broadacre City (1970)

Lionel March

Of the hundreds of designs created by Wright during his life-time, probably none has received such adverse criticism over such an extended period of time as Broadacre City. Some crit-ics, of course, took the design seriously, yet often emphasized its impracticality. The majority merely jested, calling it Wright's repository for unexecuted architectural projects and a device for attracting attention to his unorthodox social, eco-nomic, and political ideas. However, Lionel March, a social his-torian from Britain, saw many of Wright's ideas as common to the intellectual circles of the time, and that Wright was the one person capable of interpreting, in Broadacre City, the environ-mental consequences of such ideas.

March's theme, insofar as it explores sources and possible in-fluences, is akin to many articles of the forties and early fifties, previously discussed, except that it postdates them by twenty years and still lacks follow-up studies that analyze and percep-tively evaluate the designed form. From this we can perhaps

Courtesy of Lionel March. These previously unpublished talks were broadcast over the British Broadcasting Corporation's Third Programme on January 7 and 15, 1970.

infer that the urban historian is even slower than the architec-
tural critic in coming to grips with Wright.

Broadacre evolved during the early thirties, soon after Wright
established the Taliesin Fellowship. Yet its lineage dates from
early in his career. As embodied in a model, as well as draw-
ings, Broadacre City is depicted as a four-square-mile seg-
ment of America, an indefinitely expandable grid, wherein all
residential, industrial, and social amenities are represented,
and where each person or family has a tillable acre of land
(figures 29–30).

To my mind, there can be no doubt of the central significance
of Broadacre to the last thirty years of Wright's architectural
output. No proper understanding of his architectural contribution of those years can be made until his aspirations for the
emergent city are appreciated. Wright always argued that
good architecture developed out of a profound appreciation of
the life and times, the practices and ideals of the society in
which the architect lived. By Wright's own organic philosophy,
if we dismiss Broadacre, we must also dismiss his late buildings, his mature life, and his teachings. Most critics prefer to
treat Wright "inorganically," separating out his architectural
mastery over materials and space which they take seriously,
from his views of politics, economics, and social philosophy
which they judge to be eccentric and somewhat trivial. But,
contrary to the impression given by Wright's critics, these
views were in fact shared by some of the most notable intellectuals and practicing politicians of his day.

In particular I have in mind those social reformers, progressives and liberals of his day whom he "read and respected," or
whom he knew as friends. People such as William James and
John Dewey, the American pragmatists; Henry George the
popular economist; two of John Maynard Keynes'
"heretics"—C. H. Douglas and Silvio Gesell—as well as the

American institutional economists Thorstein Veblen and John Commons and the economic historian Charles Beard; in industry Henry Ford and Owen D. Young (of General Electric); in politics the "Wisconsin Idea" progressives, the La Folettes; and in social matters, Jane Addams, Edward Ross, and Richard Ely.

All of them are at once idealistic and people of action. Some are more idealistic than others, some more practical. I shall attempt to show, at least in the context of this particular liberal milieu, that Wright's views of society were unexceptionable and that in Broadacres, Wright was attempting as the *best* architect of his day to give potential architectural and urban form to what he believed to be the best thoughts and the best social actions of his American contemporaries. Most of what Wright says about society can be traced in the work, writings, and actions of these men and women. It is through them that I shall attempt to describe what Wright understood by democracy.

I think it is clear from his own writings and those of his contemporaries that he did not consider democracy to be a *form* of government, so much as a *way* of living. This distinction between *form* on the one hand and *way* or process on the other was a preoccupation of American pragmatic philosophy at the turn of the century. And it is one that we shall need to bear in mind in discussing Wright's view of the city. In contrast to the systematic philosophies of the established old world, the pragmatists conceived of an open-ended approach to cope with an entirely new and emergent situation: the humanization—as they liked to call it—of a vast continental wilderness; the construction of new settlements, of transportation and communication networks; the accelerating development of scientific knowledge and industrial power; the accumulation of unprecedented wealth; the dissemination of the pluralistic values of a polyglot people.

The pragmatists claimed that the proper purpose of social institutions—such as government, industry, schools—is to set free and develop every individual into "the full stature of his possibility." In a democracy, the pragmatic measure of all political, economic and industrial arrangements is the contribution that they make to the all-round growth of every member of society. But this is not a one-way affair. Democracy as a way

of life, John Dewey suggested, meant no less than the participation of every mature person in the formation of the values
that regulate the living of people together: and that this is as
necessary for the full development of individuals as it is for
the growth of general social welfare. Dewey, with Wright, accepted that modern industrial science and communication
technologies were the potential means by which this democracy might be physically achieved: both rejected any return to
the simple life, to some ideal but bygone Republic such as Jefferson's.

In this Wright was supported by the economic historian
Charles A. Beard, one of the most hard-headed yet influential
reform intellectuals of his generation. Beard, in his writings,
exposed the conflicts of economic interests underlying the political history of the United States from its agricultural begin-
nings to its domination by industry. Wright's vehement attacks
on big business and bankers, his conviction that the credit system leads to over-production and consequently to either unemployment or militarism and imperialism are all given
credibility in Beard's analysis of American history, as they are
indeed in Thorstein Veblen's work.

Veblen and Wright were both born into Wisconsin farming
families, and they both experienced Chicago during the nine-
ties. Veblen's iconoclastic *Theory of the Leisure Class* published in 1899 relates the expression of wealth to society in the
same way that Wright's lectures at this time compare architectural form to social function. Wright's general assumption that
capital controls industry to the detriment of the consumer was
upheld by Veblen, both believed that modern industrial resources could release men from drudgery but for usury and
the price spiral, both argued that a community that lived close
to the soil could surpass the most advanced technical nations
controlled by absentee ownership and finance, both despised
speculation in real estate, both pointed to the conspicuous
waste of salesmanship. But whereas critics take Veblen's
barbs seriously, Wright is thought to be merely crankish in
these matters.

Charles Beard and Thorstein Veblen between them summed
up what many radical and progressive intellectuals believed to
be the cause of depressions, unemployment, increasing pro-

duction but decreasing wages, and the relation of monopoly capitalism to war, but they did not provide answers to the problems. However, they both made it clear that the causes were attributable to many factors, and that the solutions must necessarily grow out of society and its institutions and that no simple remedy was available. Wright accepts this view, and at a time when many other creative intellectuals were persuaded by one economic doctrine or another, credit ought to be given him for this. His pragmatic distrust of single-minded "systems" served him well.

This is not to say that he was unaware of some of the simplistic economic panaceas which acquired popularity during the first thirty or so years of this century. He certainly knew about the "single-tax" proposals of Henry George: that just one tax—a tax on land—would effectively eliminate poverty amid progress. However, Wright rejected "single-tax" as an instant solution, while accepting the principle of communal control of land through some form of taxation.

Similarly Wright was sympathetic to C. H. Douglas's attack on economic centralization and his goal of industrial co-ownership. Both Wright and Major Douglas used the metaphor of a social pyramid balanced on an apex of monopoly capitalism, which will continue to be unstable until it is turned upside down to stand upon a broad base of popular capitalism, or economic democracy. Wright, however, was open-minded about Douglas's social credit as a solution, preferring to speak of some form of taxation which might effectively *socialize* credit.

Henry George was certain that the cause of poverty amid progress was due to the *rents* which landowners demanded, and Douglas saw its roots in the *concentrated ownership* of capital and the burden of interest. The economist who tackled both problems, land and capital together, was the German writer Silvio Gesell "whose work," John Maynard Keynes wrote, "contains flashes of deep insight and who only just failed to reach down to the essence of the matter . . . the future will learn more from the spirit of Silvio Gesell than from that of Karl Marx". It is from Gesell that Wright acquires the terms that he uses in *The Living City*: "free-land" and "free-money," currency that loses value with time, so that holders are en-

couraged to use it as soon as possible as a medium of exchange. Irving Fisher, the outstanding American economist,
writing on booms and depressions in 1933, thought that Gesell's proposal offered the speediest way out of the great
depression, and that in the long run it would be the best regu-
lator of monetary velocity. During the early thirties free-money
was realized in a number of local situations in America, and in
1933 a bill was presented to both Houses of Congress direct-
ing the Federal Treasury to issue a billion dollars worth of free-
money. So this idea, which Wright accepted for his Broadacre
proposal, was in its time and place a practical political and
economic proposition.

But Gesell's ideas would have come as no surprise to Wright
who may have heard of them by way of his friend and client
Owen D. Young who was U.S. representative at international
monetary meetings where, according to Irving Fisher, he was
actively promoting Gesellian ideas. They would simply have
confirmed the aims which pragmatic progressives were
creating through experiment and experience within states
like Wisconsin. One man in particular stands out. He is John
R. Commons, "the grand old man of the University of Wisconsin," as Wright describes his friend in his autobiography. Commons was chief among a number of scholars at the University
who charted the remarkable course of progressive reform in
Wisconsin. He was economic adviser to Robert La Follette
who distinguished himself as Governor of Wisconsin for many
years before running as Progressive candidate for Presidency
in the 1924 election. Alongside Thorstein Veblen and Wesley
Mitchell (of "business-cycle" fame), Commons had been identified by American economic historians as one of the three
most significant so-called "institutional economists" of the
early decades of this century. Commons himself defined institutional economics as "collective action for the control, liberation and the expansion of individual action." In fact he gives
an economic interpretation of the pragmatists' aim to foster
through social organization the development of every individual to "the full stature of his possibilities."

Commons, like La Follette and his other academic advisers,
had no grand design. They were against holistic systems and
theories and in favor of practical engagement and experience,
for piece-meal improvement wherever and whenever men

More Recent Evaluation

were ready to be persuaded to take a step forward. This slow but sure method of reform, in which all parties could see the reasonableness of the measures enacted, had established the Wisconsin administration by the late twenties as the most enlightened and humane in the whole of the United States. Such was the "Wisconsin idea." Not a credo, but a manner of working with people.

By the late twenties "Old Bob" La Follette was dead. His eldest son, "Young Bob," became the Senator for Wisconsin in Washington at the age of thirty, and his second son Phil succeeded to the governorship of Wisconsin, having been—and this is very significant—the secretary of Frank Lloyd Wright Incorporated, the legal body for which Wright worked. In 1934 the two La Follettes broke away from the Republican Party, which their father had skillfully bent to radical ends, to form the Progressive Party, and in the fall election both Young Bob and Phil were re-elected on the Progressive ticket. Both worked closely with Roosevelt and New Deal policies, but they vigorously opposed America's preparations for the second world war as their father had done in the first.

The progressives were: for the right of men and women to own their homes, their farms and their places of employment but against corporate and absentee ownership; for the public ownership of all utilities of common necessity including the media of energy supply and waste disposal, the media of communication—radio, telephone, post—mass and bulk transportation, and the medium of exchange (the progressives stood for the national control of the country's banking business); they were for full social security, free educational and health services; for co-operative marketing of food; for the right of workers to organize as they choose. The program was designed to recover the essential ideals of the American constitution for a broad-based democracy in a world dominated by vast corporate interests and industrial enterprises.

This is the very program Wright adopts for Broadacre City, which appeared in public for the first time one year after the progressive platform was promoted. The Progressive's political and economic program was pragmatic and radical. Broadacre City is also a radical document: it is a direct assault on the classical theory of the city in a way that Le Corbusier's work, or the Garden City movement, were not. But perhaps the most pragmatic fact about Wright's contribution to architectural theories of urban form is that he accepts that, first and foremost, a city is not an arrangement of roads, buildings, and spaces, it is a society in action. "Society" he said—"the living city." The city is a process, rather than a form. In as much as the *physical* form of the city contains the processes of democratic society it was essential, Wright argued, that it too, like the economic and political systems, contributed to the growth of every individual to the full stature of his possibilities.

Rarely have the environmental consequences of a radical social and economic program been so clearly projected as in Broadacre City. To my mind, Broadacre is one of the most brilliant examples of what is today described as "futuristics"—the study of possible futures—applied to man's environment.

Although many urbanists mistake criticism of the city by intellectuals, including William James, John Dewey, Jane Addams, and Frank Lloyd Wright, as implying rejection of the city, this is not so. Their criticism was especially vehement because these people were in love with the city as a way of life. They found in existing cities much stimulation and enjoyment, but they recognized that the majority of the people who lived in cities were oppressed and unable to develop a full sense of life. The solution to the problem was to be found through searching for a new ideal of the city, not through abandoning it. As Wright wrote:

I do not believe in a 'back to the land' movement; I think that any backward movement would be folly; but if, turning away from excess urbanization now, we can go forward with all that science has provided us, going forward intelligently to the new free forms which must be made for the accommodation of life so that it may live more generously, more spaciously and more fully, we shall be dealing—practically—with the problem now on our hands. . . . Broadacre City is the country itself come alive as a truly *great city*.

Broadacre City with its homes dispersed and disappearing into the landscape, its mixture of agricultural land and industrial plants, may not look like a city as we know cities today. But here the pragmatist's distinction that I have mentioned before between *form* and *process* is relevant. The existing city is mostly the shell of historic urban life: it reflects the lives of our forebears in many more ways than it does our own. Alfred North Whitehead in his book *Modes of Thought* writes, "If we insist on construing the new epoch in terms of the forms of order in its predecessor we see more confusion." The very words we use confirm Whitehead's point that we see in these new forms mere confusion: they are "sprawling," "sporadic," "chaotic," they despoil and erode the countryside. We see in them a process which is frustrating the "dominant order," as Whitehead called it. We fail to see the new patterns of urbanization as positive forms in their own right because we attempt to construe them in terms of our habitual assumptions derived from the past.

And so in 1930 Wright looked at the shanty squalor of gas stations posted along unmetalled tracks, and to the speculative roadside markets, which were little more than sheds surrounded by parking lots when they first appeared in the South West and especially around Los Angeles.

As he said in the thirties, the drive-in shopping centers of the future are already appearing in embryo. Even if neglected and despised, they are fingers pointing to the end of centralization. "In our present gasoline service station you may see," Wright wrote, "a crude beginning to such important advance decentralization; also see the beginning of the future humane establishment we are now calling the free city. Wherever service stations are located naturally," he goes on, "these now so often ugly and seemingly insignificant features will survive and expand." The new city "is already here all around us in the haphazard making, the apparent forces to the contrary notwithstanding. All about us and no plan. The old order is breaking up."

The democratic way of planning, as understood by Wright and the pragmatists generally, is essentially experimental and tolerant. As Wright wrote at the end of his autobiography: "The long view is the cool view. Tolerance, experiment, and change gives a culture strength."

There is, as John Dewey explained, a difference between the *planned* society and the *continuously planning* society. One requires fixed blueprints imposed from above and therefore involving reliance upon physical and psychological forces to secure conformity to them. "The other," Dewey emphasizes, "means the release of intelligence through the widest form of cooperative give-and-take. This is an operative method of activity, not a predetermined set of final truths." Unfortunately Wright's critics have failed to acknowledge that Broadacre City does not represent in any way a proposed plan, a fixed formal arrangement. This is precisely what Broadacre is not about. "To begin with," Wright states, "I believe that a general outline of any ideal is better than a specific plan or model of its particular features. An ideal once clearly fixed in mind—and the plan will come naturally enough. Fresh undertakings then appear and proceed from generals to particulars with the necessary techniques peculiar to each. But I am not trying to prove a case," says Wright, "my interest lies in sincerely appraising elemental changes I see existing or surely coming."

"Nothing to my mind," Wright wrote in 1914, "could be a worse imposition than to have some individual, even temporarily, deliberately fix the outward forms of his concept of beauty upon the future of a free people or even a growing city. A tentative, advantageous forecast of probable future utilitarian development goes far enough in this direction. Any individual willing to undertake more would thereby only prove his unfitness for the task, assuming the task possible or desirable."

Such an attitude requires tolerance to allow events to happen, but it demands outspoken criticism—no more, no physical prevention—of actions that are disapproved of. The position is an educational process, not an administrative convenience. The best analogy I can think of to describe Broadacre is to compare it with a school, not any school but the experimental kind that John Dewey ran at the University of Chicago, the kind that Froebel had called a Kindergarten and which served as the basis for the progressive Hillside School that Wright's aunts used to run. Dewey saw the school as a microcosm of democratic society. The teacher assists but does not shape the development and growth of each child. The teacher helps the child to adjust to its environment, not by accommodating itself to a fixed, a given environment, but by adjusting the factors of environment one to another in the interest of life. This involves active involvement not passive acceptance. It is no exaggeration, I suggest, that Wright partly used the term Broadacre City as Froebel had used the term Kindergarten.

More Recent Evaluation

Wright held the educational reformer in high regard. Froebel had invented the word Kindergarten, garden of children, to imply an environment wherein the child, like a plant, might be nurtured. Wright's Broadacre City is conceived similarly, as an environment to nurture citizens through the active participation and the mutual development of individuals and groups. Broadacre City, then, a garden of citizens, the city seen as community.

But how does this garden grow? The distinguished Chicago sociologist, William Ogburn, who was the Director of Research to President Hoover's Committee on Social Trends, writes that, "Success is more likely to come to those who work for and with a social trend than those who work against." This combines the Jeffersonian attitude that collectively the people in a free democracy are usually more right than any one individual, with certain Taoist ideas about the *way* of life which Wright accepted. "But should our principles dictate," Ogburn notes, "that we work against social trends we would do well to appraise the size of the effort needed, unless we wish to be martyrs. This should be heeded," he says, "by city and national planners. They should not start with a utopian urge and a clean slate. Rather they should see what the trends are. Only then can they approach realistically the task of planning." Nothing could be a clearer statement of Wright's own position.

During the last thirty years of his life Wright and his clients were building Broadacre City whenever and wherever the opportunity arose. This is, perhaps, the most audacious of Wright's attitudes towards planning. His city is not laid out on a self-contained site like Pullman, the Garden Cities or the New Towns, but it is built spot-like throughout the existing environment, each building a center of excellence and influence.

It is a process of this kind that Ogburn calls "diffusion." That diffusion works is shown by a survey on house-building in the prairie town of Oskaloosa in Iowa. Two Frank Lloyd Wright houses were built in the district in 1951. Over 9,000 people trekked out to look at them. According to a *House and Home* survey "more than a third of the visitors went back for a second look and what they saw started a home building revolution in Oskaloosa." It gave strength to people to be less conventional. It showed them how to set their houses into the rolling hills—as one new house-owner put it, "I don't think we realized until we saw these homes that we were literally shaving off the beauty of our town by grading down the sites." The two houses helped set off a chain reaction of trading-up; of people moving into new houses, of others moving into better old homes.

It is true that much of what Wright said and did challenges conventional wisdom. But we should remember those words of Blake that Wright knew so well: without contraries there can be no progress. There is much good sense in his thought, and even if we disagree we would do well to heed his criticism. Few will disagree, however, that his great contribution has been to show us how to build so as to enhance the landscape rather than to intrude upon it. Only as that lesson is learnt through action, by experiment, and with tolerance will Broadacre emerge as the dominant pattern, and will the individual, and society as a whole, become the guardians of the natural environment, masters of the technological and makers of a truly democratic culture. Where these ideals are alive, there is Broadacre.

Bibliographic Note

This bibliography is divided into three major sections in order to facilitate its use. First, Wright's own most important writings, then biographies on him, and finally a supplementary list of items relating to each of the five parts of the present book. Anyone seeking a more extensive bibliography is referred to Robert L. Sweeney's *Frank Lloyd Wright: An Annotated Bibliography* (Los Angeles, 1978) with its more than two thousand entries arranged in chronological order. And for those wishing a guide to his executed buildings, including a small snapshot of each, there is William Allin Storrer's *The Architecture of Frank Lloyd Wright: A Complete Catalogue* (Cambridge, Massachusetts, 1974; second edition, 1978).

Wright's Writings

Anyone who is interested in Frank Lloyd Wright should read *An Autobiography* (1932; updated edition, 1943; revised edition, New York, 1977) and *The Future of Architecture* (New York, 1953), the latter being an anthology that includes, among other writings, a few excerpts from his autobiography. The same is true for *The Natural House* (New York, 1954). Additional autobiographical material will be found in *A Testament* (New York, 1957). Other anthologies include those edited by Frederick Gutheim (*Frank Lloyd Wright on Architecture: Selected Writings, 1894–1940*, New York, 1941), Edgar Kaufmann (*An American Architecture*, New York, 1955), and Edgar Kaufmann and Ben Raeburn (*Frank Lloyd Wright: Writings and Buildings*, New York, 1960).

Biographies and Architectural Histories

Some of the best and most useful accounts treat only a portion of Wright's career. The basic book, although it covers only the period up to 1942, is Henry-Russell Hitchcock's *In the Nature of Materials* (New York, 1942; new edition, 1973). For the early, prairie years, there is Grant C. Manson's *Frank Lloyd Wright to 1910* (New York, 1958) and, for the entire movement in which Wright participated at that time, my book, *The Prairie School: Frank Lloyd Wright and His Midwest Contemporaries* (Toronto, 1972; New York, 1976). And for Wright's late, medium-priced residential architecture see John Sergeant's *Frank Lloyd Wright's Usonian Houses* (New York, 1976).

Full-length biographies (all entitled *Frank Lloyd Wright*) include a short and stimulating book by Vincent Scully (New York, 1960), a more provocative account by Norris Kelly Smith that, however, terminates in the 1930s (Englewood Cliffs, 1966), a study by Robert C. Twombly that emphasizes biography rather than architecture (New York, 1973; revised edition, 1979), and a more evenly balanced (between life and buildings) story by Peter Blake (1960; Baltimore and Harmondsworth, 1964).

For anyone seeking chiefly illustrations there is, alas, nothing comparable to Le Corbusier's *Oeuvre Complete*. The best source remains Hitchcock's *In the Nature of Materials* in spite of its 1942 cut-off date, and for Wright's drawings and unexecuted projects there is Arthur Drexler's *The Drawings of Frank Lloyd Wright* (New York, 1962).

Other Writings on Wright
For part I, Wright's Personality and Life Style, refer to my preceding discussion on biographies.

To part II, His Clients and His Work, other readings might include the entire National Trust for Historic Preservation booklet about *The Pope-Leighey House* (Helen D. Bullock and Terry B. Morton, eds., Washington, D.C., 1969) from which I have taken several excerpts, the exemplary (and inexpensive) book by Donald Hoffmann on *Frank Lloyd Wright's Fallingwater* (New York, 1978), Herbert Jacobs's account of *Building with Frank Lloyd Wright* (San Francisco, 1978), and a forthcoming book by Paul R. and Jean S. Hanna (The MIT Press) concerning their California home. Also central to this theme is Leonard K. Eaton, *Two Chicago Architects and Their Clients: Frank Lloyd Wright and Howard Van Doren Shaw* (Cambridge, Massachusetts, 1969).

Concerning part III, American Assessment, one should mention the two *House Beautiful* articles about Wright's Oak Park home and studio published in volume 1, February 1897, and volume 7, December 1899, the short note in *Architectural Record* (vol. 18, July 1905) on "Work of Frank Lloyd Wright, Its Influence" which was really a filler while *AR* editors awaited a longer commissioned piece (see my explanation, page 83), Thomas E. Tallmadge "The 'Chicago School'" (*Architectural Review* (Boston) 15, April 1908), and "A Departure from the Classic Tradition: Two Unusual Houses by Louis Sullivan and Frank Lloyd Wright" (*Architectural Record* 30, October 1911). When the Imperial Hotel failed to collapse during the Tokyo earthquake of 1923 Wright was momentarily thrust into the limelight. This resulted in his belated listing in *Who's Who* and in the publication of several reports concerning the hotel including two by Louis H. Sullivan (*Architectural Record*, vols. 53, April 1923, and 55, February 1924).

Bibliographic Note

In the introduction to part IV, European Discovery, I listed various works that might be read, yet many of them are neither readily available nor in English. The best additional source, mostly in English, is *The Life-Work of the American Architect Frank Lloyd Wright* of 1925 (new edition, New York, 1965) which includes texts by Berlage, Mallet-Stevens, Mendelsohn, Oud, and Wijdeveld (the editor) as well as by Lewis Mumford, Sullivan, and Wright.

Part V, More Recent Evaluation, must begin with those works that so nearly formed the basis of this book (see Introduction and its footnote), specifically Henry-Russell Hitchcock, "Frank Lloyd Wright and the 'Academic Tradition'" (*Journal of the Warburg and Courtauld Institutes* 7, January–June 1944), Dimitri Tselos, "Exotic Influences in the Architecture of Frank Lloyd Wright" (*Magazine of Art* 46, April 1953)—and his follow-up article, "Frank Lloyd Wright and World Architecture" (*Journal of the Society of Architectural Historians* 28, March 1969), Grant C. Manson, "Wright in the Nursery" (*Architectural Review* 113, London, June 1953), and Vincent Scully, *The Shingle Style* (New Haven, 1955). Also to be added is David Gebhard's "A Note on the Chicago Fair of 1893 and Frank Lloyd Wright" (*Journal of the Society of Architectural Historians* 18, May 1959).

Supplemental reading relating to the specific topics presented in part V would include the following: for Richard C. MacCormac's article one might add his own "Froebel's Kindergarten Gifts and the Early Work of Frank Lloyd Wright" (*Environment and Planning B*, vol. 1, no. 1, 1974) and John Sergeant's "Woof and Warp: a Spatial Analysis of Frank Lloyd Wright's Usonian Houses" (*Environment and Planning B*, vol. 3, no. 2, 1976). The most sympathetic appreciation of Wright's space (although its construction is not analyzed) is Peter Blake's "Frank Lloyd Wright: Master of Architectural Space" (*Architectural Forum* 109, September 1958) while the best additional literature on Broadacre City is George R. Collin's article in *Four Great Makers of Modern Architecture* (New York, 1963) or Robert C. Twombly's "Undoing the City: Frank Lloyd Wright's Planned Communities" (*American Quarterly* 24, October 1972).

Illustrations

Figure 1 William Winslow house, River Forest, Illinois, 1894. Shown in relation to the elm tree that helped determine the character of the house. (Courtesy Museum of Modern Art)

Figure 2 William Winslow house. Detail of plaster frieze. (Photo by author)

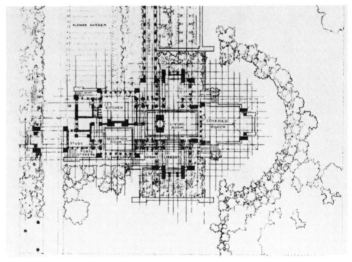

Figure 3 Darwin D. Martin house, Buffalo, New York, 1904 (Courtesy Buffalo and Erie County Historical Society)

Figure 4 Darwin D. Martin house. Plan: showing 4'-6" unit system drawn by Wright. (*Architectural Record*, January 1928)

Illustrations

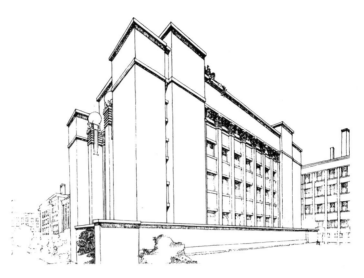

Figure 5 Larkin Administration Building, Buffalo, New York, 1904. (Wright's drawing that was published by Ernst Wasmuth in *Ausgeführte Bauten und Entwürfe von Frank Lloyd Wright*, Berlin, 1910.)

Figure 6 Larkin Administration Building. Entrance facade. (*Inland Architect and News Record*, July 1907)

Illustrations

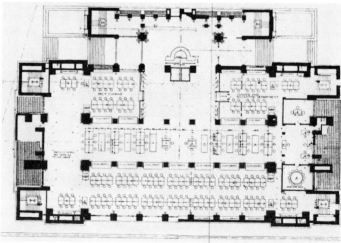

Figure 7 Larkin Administration Building. Interior. (Courtesy Henry-Russell Hitchcock)

Figure 8 Larkin Administration Building. Plan. (*Wendingen* I, 1925)

Figure 9 Unity Temple, Oak Park, Illinois, 1906. (Courtesy Museum of Modern Art)

Figure 10 Unity Temple. Interior. (Courtesy Henry-Russell Hitchcock)

Figure 11 Frederick C. Robie house, Chicago, Illinois, 1907. (Courtesy Henry-Russell Hitchcock)

Figure 12 Frederick C. Robie house. Living room looking toward dining room. (Photo by author)

Illustrations

Figure 13 Taliesin, Spring Green, Wisconsin, 1911. Courtyard looking toward entrance loggia and living room. (Courtesy Henry-Russell Hitchcock)

Figure 14 Taliesin. Dining area within living room. (Courtesy Henry-Russell Hitchcock)

Illustrations

Figure 15 View of Taliesin (right) and the original farm buildings (left) that later were converted to residential use. Photo taken from Middle Hill, halfway between Taliesin and Hillside, the latter being where the Fellowship buildings and Romeo and Juliet windmill are located. (Courtesy Henry-Russell Hitchcock)

Figure 16 Eric Mendelsohn and Frank Lloyd Wright at Taliesin. (Photo by Edgar Tafel)

Illustrations

Figure 17 Fallingwater, Bear Run, Pennsylvania, 1936. (Photo by Michael Fedison, courtesy Western Pennsylvania Conservancy)

Figure 18 Fallingwater. Living room. (Photo by Harold Corsini, courtesy Western Pennsylvania Conservancy)

Illustrations

Figure 19 Taliesin West, Scottsdale, Arizona, 1937. (Photo by author, 1956)

Figure 20 Taliesin West. (Photo by author, 1956)

Illustrations

Figure 21 Paul R. Hanna house, Stanford, California, 1936. (Photo by author)

Figure 22 Paul R. Hanna house. Living room. (Courtesy Henry-Russell Hitchcock)

Illustrations

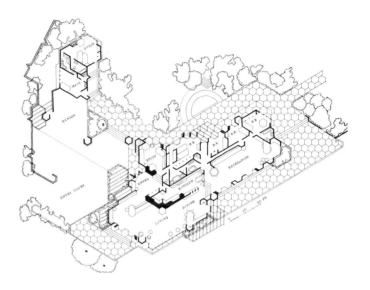

Figure 23 Paul R. Hanna house. Plan, 1936. (Courtesy Museum of Modern Art)

Figure 24 Melwyn M. Smith house, Bloomfield Hills, Michigan, 1946. (Photo by Donald G. Kalec)

Illustrations

Figure 25 Loren Pope house, Mount Vernon, Virginia, 1939. Interior. (Photo by Jack Boucher, courtesy HABS)

Figure 26 Loren Pope house. Plan. (Courtesy National Trust for Historic Preservation)

Illustrations

Figure 27 Beth Shalom Synagogue, Elkins Park, Pennsylvania, 1954. (Photo by Jacob Stelman, courtesy Beth Shalom Congregation)

Figure 28 Marin County Civic Center and Administration Building, San Rafael, California, designed 1957, constructed posthumously. (Photo by author)

Figure 29 (top right) Broadacre City, project, begun 1934. (Courtesy Museum of Modern Art)

Figure 30 (bottom right) Broadacre City. Schematic diagram—which may also serve as a key to figure 29. (Courtesy Museum of Modern Art)

Illustrations

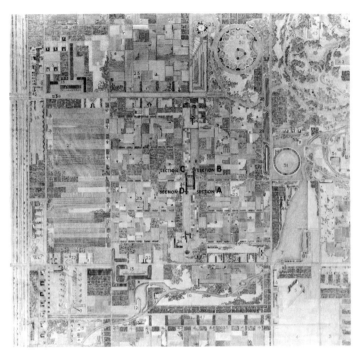

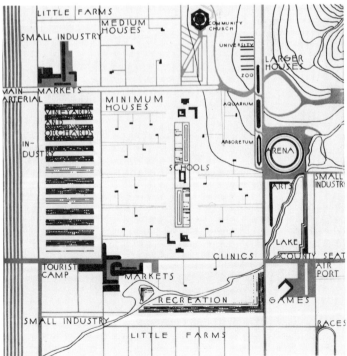

Index

Numerals in italics refer to illustrations.